The Unknown
Shore

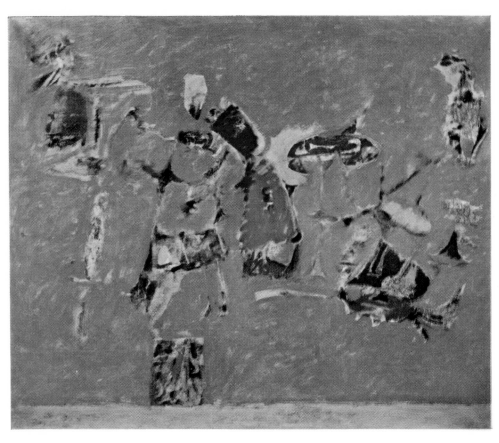

ARSHILE GORKY, *Untitled,* 1943-1948. Oil, 54½ x 64½.

(*Courtesy of Sidney Janis Gallery, New York*)

The Unknown Shore: A VIEW

OF CONTEMPORARY ART

by Dore Ashton

An Atlantic Monthly Press Book

Little, Brown and Company · Boston · Toronto

ATLANTIC–LITTLE, BROWN BOOKS
ARE PUBLISHED BY
LITTLE, BROWN AND COMPANY
IN ASSOCIATION WITH
THE ATLANTIC MONTHLY PRESS

Published simultaneously in Canada
by Little, Brown & Company (Canada) Limited

PRINTED IN THE UNITED STATES OF AMERICA

for
ADJA
and
ALEXANDRA

I have found myself caught between two ages as in the conflux of two rivers, and I have plunged into their waters, turning regretfully from the old bank upon which I was born, yet swimming hopefully toward the unknown shore at which the new generations are to land.

— Chateaubriand

Preface

ALL GREAT SYSTEMS of art criticism, all methods invented for distinguishing style, have been created by scholars looking back. Their simplifications occur only in retrospect and are imposed by minds that have selected the material to be classified. Sometimes selection is governed by a vivid temperament that through its creative force can make one style, one aspect of art, seem singularly important.

Heinrich Wölfflin, one of the most inspired art historians, understood very well when painters objected to his classifying technique. But in order to give form and style to his own speculations, he had to insist that "the course of the development of art cannot be simply reduced to a series of separate points . . . that is to say: to the personal style must be added the style of the school, country and race."

The critic attempting to deal with contemporary art, however, is obliged to regard the artist as a separate point, since there are no established definitions of school, country and race. Although he can trace obvious lines of descent and find relationships with work of the past, his clearest approach can be only through contemplation of the individual artist's work.

Art criticism is not a science but an application of intelligent discussion. The attempt to define, rather than the definition itself, is its justification. There is an element of truth in any searching discussion of art if it serves to focus close attention on the work of art.

Baudelaire was the first modern critic who fully realized the necessity of regarding the contemporary artist as a separate point in order to characterize his special genius. With brilliant imagination Baudelaire was able to isolate the central problems of his time and the future so convincingly, so presciently that his observations are still valid.

The lessons we have learned from Baudelaire — hard lessons that took a century to secure — can be simply paraphrased. Three of the most important are: The connoisseur must be cosmopolitan in his approach. Provincialism either in time or place is deadly to the perception of beauty. Second, he must never become entangled in a system. It is a kind of damnation that leads only to painful recantations. The "infinite spiral of life" will always defeat the inventor of a system and obscure from his view "the immense keyboard of universal correspondences." Third, he must cast out the notion of progress, "avoid it like the very devil." Proofs are abundant in the history of art that "every efflorescence is spontaneous, individual" at its core.

These are only three of the many points Baudelaire

made but they are enough to suggest that the twentieth century is living out an experience begun in the mid-nineteenth century. The romantic period is not yet over.

Only recently have we felt comfortable in rejecting theories of progress in the arts. Criticism has almost caught up with art itself in sacrificing the pseudoscientific craving to make every judgment fit old theories of causality. Baudelaire asked if Signorelli really begat Michelangelo, if Perugino really contained Raphael, and answered categorically that the artist stems only from himself. It has taken us a long time to put into a larger context the useful and assurance-inspiring historical approach that makes every son explainable by his father.

At least we hesitate nowadays to adopt a neat system of style determination. We have learned that dominant tendencies exist, but never do they exclude all other tendencies. Everything is always present in the body of art, but at certain times, one element may be more apparent than another.

For example, it was the habit of early twentieth-century art historians to append epithets such as logical, rational and classical to French painting. And with some justice. Yet, when the Second World War was over, a group of painters emerged in Paris who were deliberately anticlassical. Critics appeared to stress the newly emerged tendency, to scrap the old epithets. Michel Tapié talked feverishly about an *art autre* and a paradox called "the informal form-will." André Breton, surrealist magician that he was, hastily scoured history for a precedent and "discovered" Gallic coins. With their wild, asymmetrical reliefs, these coins proved to Breton's satisfaction that there had always been an endemic expressionist tradition in French art.

Breton's thesis was a pretty invention, a gross exaggeration. But it did shift the accent to contemporary art. The construction of his theory was emphatically unscientific, full of vulnerable statements, yet it served a purpose. It emphasized the resounding character of the paintings he was discussing and in its very inconsistencies provoked reflection.

In bringing fragments of history to bear on a painting of the moment Breton did not *explain* the painting. He merely added a point of departure from the circumference of the magic circle around the artist which keeps us always at a distance from the inviolable point — the work of art — at its center. Breton's farfetched reference to a cultural heritage serves as one of the many probing rays that can be sent into the center. The tissues connecting works of art will never be wholly manifest, but every analogy, every insight the viewer can bring to bear, lands him that much nearer to the vital center.

In this essay I have tried to speak mainly of what I have witnessed in both the United States and Europe after the Second World War. The conflicts, differences and convergences existing between the American and European avant-garde art interest me. So does the problematical "influence" of the cultural envelope. I see both European and American painting as stemming from the nineteenth-century romantic tradition. I see many mitigating factors — temperaments of individual artists, special local conditions, modern diffusion of philosophical ideas and scientific knowledge. I believe the perfervid romantic character of American painting has peculiarities and historical precedents that make it distinct from similar tendencies in Europe, and as I am American, I tend to work more closely with American phenomena. The special circumstances of postwar European painting — the fact alone that the war was fought in Europe — makes it distinct. At the same time, there have been general ideas unfolding from the basic romantic tradition which have conditioned both Europeans and Americans. A common trend is apparent in the undeniable accent on expressionism, or action painting. All other styles, says Sir Herbert Read, can be related more or less directly to styles that prevailed before the war.

I have speculated on the differences and problems confronted by artists after the war. I have tried to write about individual artists less with the intention of "placing" them in history than with the hope of elucidating images that are permanently installed in my imagination. My choice is arbitrary and retrospective. By examining that which has already seemed to register itself in history I have tried to approach "the unknown shore" with open eyes.

Acknowledgments

MOST of the thoughts in this book were first explored in the columns of *Arts & Architecture,* whose editor, John Entenza, is in every way an exceptional editor. I am deeply grateful to him.

I am grateful, too, to Dr. Israel Rosen, whose confidence in my work touched and inspired me.

To Dr. F. S. Licht, who read my manuscript and made invaluable suggestions, to Charlotte Devree, who did the same, and to Merloyd Lawrence my deep thanks.

Among the many friends who have in special ways shown interest in my book, I wish to thank John Brinnin, Dr. Peter Selz, Miriam Schapiro and Sylvia Ashton.

Above all I thank my husband, Adja Yunkers, a painter whose work I have admired for many years and who, under any other circumstances, would belong in this essay.

A Ford Foundation Grant enabled me to devote the time spent in writing this book.

Contents

Illustrations

I : The American Note

I : The Threat of Novelty

A NATURAL distaste for the vulgarities of the *nouveaux riches* was partly responsible for the nineteenth-century artist's defensive romantic position. Circumstance and bitter experience shaped his stubborn resistance to what he considered the encroachments of materialism and utilitarianism on his art. The word "utilitarian," pronounced scornfully, recurs in nineteenth-century literature, from Carlyle and Ruskin to Flaubert and Proust. It wasn't merely that smoke from the steam engine and refuse from factories made sensitive eyes smart. It was that industrialization and the increasingly important role of the bourgeoisie threatened the artist at every turn.

Many a young artist resisted the temptation to back himself into a romantically free and therefore isolated position at first. Baudelaire himself started out defiantly rejecting the exquisite aestheticism of the preceding romantic generation. He addressed his reviews of the salons of 1845 and 1846 to the bourgeois, the "natural friend of the arts," and declared that each book not addressed to the majority is a stupid book. "First of all," he wrote in 1845, "apropos of that impertinent appellation the bourgeois, we declare that we don't share in any way the prejudices of our great *artistic* confreres who have strived for many years to throw anathema on this inoffensive being who would ask nothing better than to love good painting, if these gentlemen knew how to make it understood and if artists showed it to him often." And he added, "The bourgeois is very respectable; one must please those at whose expense one wishes to live."

But not long after, Baudelaire had to acknowledge that this inoffensive being, the "natural lover of the arts," not only loved them for the wrong reasons, but threatened to suffocate them altogether. By 1859, and after considerable adverse personal experience, Baudelaire was inveighing against the same bourgeois in his salon, calling him a crude hyperborean that all the visions of Damask, all the thunders and lightnings in creation would not enlighten. He began to attack what appeared to be a new class of literary workers, the darlings of the bourgeoisie, sacrilegious priests of art: "There is one thing a thousand times more dangerous than the bourgeois, the *bourgeois artist* who was created to interpose himself between the public and the genius." [1]

Flaubert complained about mass production, regretting that a crowd of machine-men was growing in the factories, and a crowd of rich bourgeois was overwhelming the arts. "How many good people a century ago could have lived perfectly well without the beaux-arts, who now need little statuettes, little music and little literature!" [2]

The cry has been the same since the mid-nineteenth century: mass democracy leads to popularization, and popularization is the enemy of the independent artist. Baudelaire said so in his impassioned introduction to the works of Edgar Allan Poe, whom he considered stifled by a democratic society. "A pitiless dictatorship is that of opinion in democratic societies; don't beg of it either charity, or indulgence or elasticity in the application of its laws to the multiple and complex problems of spiritual life." [3]

The demands of the bourgeoisie were reflected in the rise and industrialization of the popular press. No longer the dignified and sequestered journal of literary criticism and lofty political discussion, the newspaper became purveyor of a little bit of everything. So-called critics praised the pretty paintings in the salons designed for the growing bourgeois market; praised the sentimental novels written expressly to be serialized and paid by the line; praised the theaters where popular entertainment was offered (and which were advertised in the newly established columns of publicity) and successfully crowded out thoughtful littérateurs who formerly had served the press at a high level.

Sensitive artists watching all this had little choice. A posture of aloofness was indispensable to their artistic integrity. The novelties demanded insatiably by the restless middle classes must at all costs be recognized for what they were: ephemeral, flattering images of the bourgeoisie itself.

The conflict was by no means easy to support. The public, after all, was indispensable to the artist. Sometimes he had to relent, to accept the praise of the mass, to feed — perhaps unconsciously — its tapewormed innards with the new.

What was apparent to the artists of England and France at the end of the nineteenth century and beginning of the twentieth was even more galling to the American artist whose experience of the same problems was many times more brutal. Novelty and bad taste were the very essence of American society in the blooming industrial revolution. Millionaires were that much cruder, more rapacious, more "utilitarian" and overbearing. The need to find artistic identity sent American writers and painters fleeing to Europe where at least certain old institutions were still preserved. When they returned home, they were even less suited to the moral climate and often adopted attitudes far more extreme than their counterparts in Europe. Their uneasiness remained a characteristic of the American avant-garde.

Struggle as they might, artists have not been able to keep the issues clear. Inevitably, the mass has wrung certain compromises from the art world. The insistent complaints of thoughtful commentators — complaints that remain astonishingly similar over a century — have not brooked the tide. Novelty for novelty's sake has permeated culture in Europe and, much more, in the United States.

In the bulk of commentary accompanying contemporary painting, for instance, the word "new" has long since superseded the word "original." With the best of intentions journalists and critics have yearly signaled innovations. They have celebrated the new so often that the word is virtually useless in criticism. This indiscriminate quest for the new robs art of its legitimate proportions. A critical approach that disregards everything but the novel can never reveal the resonance of a work of art and renders the artist a disservice. What is worse, it promotes the false illusion that art, like fashion, is ephemeral.

2 : The Beginnings of an
American Avant-Garde

WHAT is now referred to as the "new American painting" (following the terminology of the Museum of Modern Art in speaking of the work of a few artists since the Second World War) is new only in terms of the individual originality of the painters embraced by the term.[1] The idea of a "new" painting in America is not new at all. It has come desultorily to the surface for more than fifty years. During that period, there were many vagaries of style, many digressions, but through it all, a singular avant-garde spirit, formulated in the first decade of the century, managed to survive. The romantic intransigence of European artists, transplanted to America, took on an eccentric character. Art for art's sake dicta were translated with verve and impatience in the refreshingly anarchic terms peculiar to America.

Forgetting for a moment the idea of a "new American painting," it is possible to see that the ideas hovering over the arts in 1945 — the date often given for the identification of a new American painting — were not invented but reinvented. They had been stated to a large degree as early as 1910 in New York. One has only to spend an afternoon reading back issues of *Camera Work*, the magazine edited by the photographer–art dealer Alfred Stieglitz, to see how persistent ideas can be.

In the extravagantly avant-garde pages of *Camera Work* in 1910 the ambiguities concerning space and the cosmos familiar in literature about contemporary abstract expressionism were already in evidence. Max Weber, who had followed the European avant-garde closely in Paris, had studied with Matisse and watched the beginnings of cubism, wrote in an exalted language that more sophisticated European avant-garde critics would have considered gauche and American: "In plastic art, I believe, there is a fourth dimension which may be described as the consciousness of a great and overwhelming sense of space-magnitude in all directions at one time . . . It is somewhat similar to color and depth in musical sounds."

Another writer refers to "cosmism" in painting and declares: "Art enters the morphological organism of things to know their essence." There are repeated references to the "new art" (though not the new *American* art — in those days the spirit was rather more international). The stress is on philosophical abstractions even when they seem only remotely related to the works Stieglitz was exhibiting in his gallery. Writers close to what was then the vanguard in American painting extolled its unorthodoxy in a diction resembling current diction in *Art News,* or in the New York artists' house organ, *It Is.*

The parallels are many. In the 1912 issues of *Camera Work* the critics seemed preoccupied with science in the same ambivalent way critics are today. With indiscriminate enthusiasm, they fell upon new scientific principles that appeared to contradict the positivism inherited from the nineteenth century. At the same time, they liked to assert the superiority of artistic intuition. Einstein's first paper on relativity had been published in 1905, but writers in *Camera Work* were not really concerned with it. Rather, like painters then as now, they intuitively sensed the broad general shift in scientific thought and used isolated axioms (probably erroneously from the scientific point of view) to confirm discoveries they had made within their own work.

The tendency persists today. Since no one has developed a rhetoric for criticism of contemporary abstract painting, there is a certain embarrassment of language which leads painters and writers to borrow terms from science to justify the products of their nonscientific processes. We find time-space continua, improbabilities, mathematical topologies and infinite numbers drawn rather loosely into aesthetic discussions. Yet somehow, these phrases become incantatory, conjuring a climate, a special mantle for the sciences and the arts.

As the words of Max Weber indicate, the commentators in the early issues of *Camera Work* were all for an

art freed from classical, geometrically logical space ideas.
Their idea of a free painting came remarkably close to
what is now called "abstract expressionism" or "informalism." Like the contemporary informal or abstract expressionist painter, they had a strong respect for the element
of chance in creation. They described the "new art" as "the
apotheosis of the intuitive" and believed that random activity could be the source of revelation. Also like the in-
formalist today, they swept tradition aside to encounter
a *tabula rasa* on which their intuition could play.

The avant-garde movement then was perhaps more
ebullient, and certainly more confident than it is today. A
writer in a 1913 issue of *Camera Work* didn't hesitate to
list three definite postulates of the "new movement":

(1) An infinite world of experience.

(2) A man spiritually free from social conventions.

(3) An art free because devoid of concrete limitations.

One of the most avid writers of the day, Benjamin de
Casseres, triumphantly rid himself of nineteenth-century
materialistic theory and plunged back as far as Heraclitus
for his aesthetics. He expounded a shaky theory of aesthetic flux, declaring, "There is no unity but the unity of
each sensation, each emotion."

The autonomy of the unit de Casseres insisted on still
interests painters, as I will show later. By 1913 all the arts
seemed to have moved toward the episodic and fragmentary. The lyrical principal, still reigning, was already established. Mondrian was soon to react fruitfully against what
he labeled the "lyrical principle" which he felt contained

the principles of tragedy and chaos — two elements that exclude a "pure plastic language." But American painters relished chaos and tragedy as sources of imagery.

They were early attracted to the riches of the stream of consciousness. Painters who visited France knew of Bergson's *Creative Evolution* (1907). His lectures at the Sorbonne were widely discussed in artistic milieux. The stream of consciousness, that in its Bergsonian interpretation swept up all the fragments of life and laid them out in completely unorthodox, seemingly disorganized schema, held a powerful appeal for the impatient American spirits. *Camera Work* theorists determined that the conventional unities of previous art epochs were incompatible with "modern" life. It was the "experimental" aspect of painting that was important — the flow of sensations and intimations of the "infinite world of experience." It was a short step for the experimental approach as they defined it to become identified with the very act of painting, the gesture that gave us the term "action painting."

Although the American avant-garde before the First World War was tutored by the European — Arthur Dove, Alfred Maurer and Max Weber had all visited Paris before 1910 — its proclamations were markedly biased in favor of the "instinctual principle." Though even such imaginative writers as Guillaume Apollinaire and Max Jacob tempered their art commentaries with specific analyses of paintings and tried to speak in terms of the structure and painterly virtue of the new painting, the Americans blithely ignored specific analysis. Theirs was an ebullient,

idealistic and abstract approach. There was no time to pin
down theories.

It is significant that a direct European contribution to Stieglitz's circle came from Francis Picabia, a renegade cubist who, together with Marcel Duchamp, stirred up New York's intelligentsia with wild and fanciful tirades. Picabia, in a 1913 issue of *Camera Work,* published an essay titled "Toward Amorphism" in which he declared "war on form" and twitted the public for its hidebound notions of representation in painting. Stieglitz's choice of texts was unerringly offbeat. It was he who first published Kandinsky in English in 1912, presenting an excerpt from *On the Spiritual in Art,* known at the time to only a tiny minority in Germany, where it had just been published. (It wasn't translated into French until 1949.)

On the whole, the painters and writers around Stieglitz were keenly interested in European ideas, followed developments in Europe closely and were not reluctant to be influenced. Stieglitz's early exhibitions of works by Picasso, Matisse and Rodin stimulated the American painters who frequented his gallery and prepared them for their own battle with an indifferent public. The artists of Stieglitz's circle did their best to broadcast the significance of the changed course of American painting, the result of the 1913 Armory Show.[2] They were satisfied to have been raked by the gusty winds of European change.

The extent of the continuing European influence and the steady interchange of ideas between American and European artists can be judged by the worried and at times hysterical commentaries in the American art press. The rage of the archreactionary Royal Cortissoz, writing for the *New York Tribune,* indicates a small measure of the adverse reaction Stieglitz and his coterie produced. Cortissoz had been an opponent from the beginning. It used to amuse Stieglitz to print Cortissoz's long diatribes against the shows in his galley — exhibitions of Weber, Marin and Dove, for instance — in *Camera Work.* He also reprinted full columns by other baffled critics, without commentary. Despite the minority of avant-garde artists, they always received ample attention in the press, more attention in fact than is given today when only two New York papers carry extensive art coverage.

By 1923, Cortissoz had reached the limit of his patience and published a book in which he wrote a chapter on what he called "Ellis Island Art." In it he said that "the United States is invaded by aliens, thousands of whom constitute so many acute perils to the health of the body politic. Modernism is of precisely the same heterogeneous alien origin and is imperilling the republic of art in the same way." [3]

His response to heterogeneity and modernism was so violent that he confessed he could not even bring himself to look at the paintings in question or to listen to the exponents of the "new art."

If he and the other patriotic spokesmen for conventional painting had had the courage to take a long look at what was being done by the handful of young American painters of the "modernist" stamp, he might have detected an embarrassingly American note in the clamor.

3 • Locating the American Note:
• A Digression

LOCATING an American note is a troublesome problem. Some contemporary critics, eager to establish a national art, hear the note everywhere, even in the work of European painters who certainly had no contact with the United States while they were formulating their abstract styles. In contrast to the excessively patriotic critics are those whose ingrained habits of respect for European culture blind them to everything in America. In the full concert of recent American painting they can hear only dominant European chords.

Methodical analysis would perhaps result in a balance sheet of "American" and "alien" characteristics in contemporary painting. But this method has the disadvantage of distracting attention from the works themselves. The value of comparative criticism is not so much in making subdivisions of differences as it is in developing full, circular discussion which covers a large group of characteristics and finds common ones.

If I were trying to locate the American note in the work of Stieglitz's painters I might go back to the seventeenth and eighteenth centuries and talk about the innocence, the direct realism of the American journeyman painters, in contrast with the sophisticated artifice of the Europeans during the same period.

I might point to the landscape-painting tradition in the United States with its idiosyncratic adaptation of the romantic landscape of England; its eccentric practitioners whose training was largely acquired in nature; and its insistent reference to "place."

At the same time, I would have to note the influence of European academic painting, right through the nineteenth century. A number of America's painters were trained in Germany and brought back the "finish" provided by the academy.

In relation to Arthur Dove, these background observations might make some sense and help to determine where he differed from the European avant-garde painters, and where he stepped out of his own tradition. The series of "abstractions" he painted in 1910, based on observations of "the spirit" of nature, might then be related to recent American painting. Dove, while his paintings were more radical than those of most Europeans except perhaps Kandinsky at the time, clung to the subjects he extracted from close observation of nature. He said that modern minds were reaching out toward an art of pure color and form dissociated from representation, but he himself never sought the ultimate purity. Like his romantic abstract successors in America, he was more interested in expressing the "forces" of nature than in developing a pure, abstract art. Beyond this, if there were something specifically "American" in his work, it could only be sensed in Dove's imagery.

A digression into literature makes my point more clear. Consider William Carlos Williams's subjective prose-poem on Edgar Allan Poe in *In the American Grain*.[1] Williams locates what he thinks is peculiarly American about Poe in the course of an exultant, zigzagging commentary—but he locates it subjectively, from the inside. He enters Poe's work, steeps himself, makes short shrift of conventional attitudes marring contemplation and, from what he considers Poe's own point of view, deduces an American essence.

He describes Poe as "a genius intimately shaped by his locality and time." From this we might think he is about to apply from the outside the Tainean system of race, moment, milieu. But Williams swiftly corrects this impression, asserting that "Poe's work strikes by its scrupulous originality, *not* originality in the bastard sense, but in its legitimate sense of solidity which goes back to the ground." This nonprovable qualification of origins takes Williams's thesis out of the framework of objective analysis and puts it squarely in the subjective register.

Although Williams is bent on determining Poe's American traits, he does not analyze the institutions that existed in Poe's time. Rather, through reading Poe he has *sensed*

the "place" — sensed it as a sprawling mass of irrecon-
cilables. This is an artist's way of distinguishing place. I
have heard American painters talk about the United States
in the same abstract, emotional vein. The American painter
still regards himself as a pioneer. Williams understood the
nature of the artist's pioneer-image, writing of Poe: "His
greatness is in that he turned his back and faced inland, to
originality, with the identical gesture of a Boone." He sees
Poe seeing himself as the embattled artist (Harold Rosenberg saw the 1946 American "anti-Style" painters as Coon-
skinners).[2]

"He was the first to realize that the hard, sardonic,
truculent mass of the New World, hot, angry — was, in
fact, not a thing to paint over, to smear, to destroy — for
it WOULD not be destroyed, it was too powerful, — it
smiled! That it is NOT a thing to be slighted by men.
Difficult, its very difficulty was their strength. It was in the
generous bulk of its animal crudity that their every fine-
ness would be found safely imbedded."

When Williams returns to locality and time, he still
shies away from factual documentation. "The local causes
shaping Poe's genius were two in character: the necessity
for a fresh beginning, backed by a native vigor of extraordinary proportions — with the corollary, that all 'colonial imitation' must be swept aside."

Williams could, in fact, be speaking for the painters.
Generally speaking, the two "local causes" he finds shaping Poe's genius are the precise causes that spurred the
painters in Stieglitz's day and incited painters of our own
period.

A "fresh beginning" has been the recurrent cry of the embattled American artist. The avant-garde around Stieglitz wiped their slates clean of all nineteenth-century memories — of fashionable portraits, of plaster-cast realism, or a rigidly controlled space conception. The problem of "colonial imitation" has consistently rankled American painters. Even the most aggressive of the "new American" painters in 1945 were well aware of the omnipotence of Picasso, for instance, and were specifically on guard against his influence. The "great" painters of the twentieth century were still the Europeans, and it was apparent to each of the determined men who re-created the American avant-garde after the Second World War that only after those European shades were exorcised would there be a resurgence of originality here. In this sense, Williams's description of Poe's problems can be taken as equally accurate for any American artist.

In this digression, I try to suggest that though we will always — and naturally — be attracted by the idea that there is an American essence in our painting, it is an idea that is better kept secondary. It is more fruitful to work from the universal to the particular.

When I discuss a group of artists who happen to be American, it is understood that they have been shaped by their locality and place in time. But when they transcend locality and place in their imagery, as I think Poe did, they enter the universal realm of art. Their images are then related to human experience wherever in place and time it transpires. They can and should be related to ideas far larger than mere nationality.

4 : The Second Wave of Avant-Gardism: The 1940's

THE HISTORY of American art is relatively brief, tempestuous and laced with paradox. Finding precise "local causes" would be a difficult enterprise. Its line is full of strange interruptions and abrupt transitions. Tendencies come and go with such haste that they scarcely have time to be noted. Yet the drive for fresh beginnings has never abated.

Most of the artists working today in the uncompromising romantic tradition Williams sketches were born before 1920 into a fluid cultural situation. There was no binding tradition in American painting, but there were many unchallenged conventions. The forceful ideas sponsored by those around Stieglitz filtered through very slowly, due to this tangle of unexamined conventions, and were picked out only sporadically in the years between the wars when these painters were very young. There were a few American painters throughout that period who worked toward a synthesis of their own and European concepts. A faithful knot of cubist and abstract painters continued to function from Stieglitz's time on. But they formed a very small unit within the artists's community, and their adaptations of European styles were not always original.[1]

The paradoxes in the American art tradition account for some of the miscarried efforts of American painters to possess European styles. They had been touched by the Puritan bias of their culture. Art for the average American was still expendable, connected in his mind with other sensual occupations condemned from the beginning by the Puritan community, and suspiciously unusable. From the day most American painters first set brush to canvas, they began with the unconscious struggle against a utilitarian tradition. Their obstacles were incomparably more powerful than those the European artists faced. The hostile "society" that avant-garde writers in 1913 bade them be free of in America was composed of empirical, hardheaded men to whom the artist most often represented dissidence and even subversion.

It was such sullen hostility that caused a sensitive librarian and philanthropist, John Cotton Dana, to write a cajoling pamphlet in 1914, *American Art, How It Can Be Made to Flourish*.[2] His first chapter, wryly titled "There Is Very Little of It," explained that "we were too busy, and our rich buy art objects elsewhere." He gently observed, "We seem to have been born with the work habit but we have slight leaning yet toward that art habit which calls

for careful training of our unexpended fund of feelings."
Finally, with an indication of his exasperation, Dana
asked: If the rich called for works of art as they called for
automobiles, would not the worthy products have appeared?

Since Dana's day the rich have called and the products
appeared, but the careful training of feeling has yet to
come. Artists still labor within a largely uncomprehend-
ing society.

At the same time that the Puritan tradition presented all
kinds of problems and complexes for the American artist
— here is one of the paradoxes — there had always been a
flourishing romantic obbligato to American arts and letters. The dark stream in American literature — its contained violence, soaring idealism, protest, despair, energetic will to transcend material facts and reach a zone of
pure thought and feeling — was equally reflected in painting. Poe and Melville characterized the abiding romantic
tendency in America paralleling the European. Many of
the distinguished artists in the past two hundred years have
been fervent romanticists (Albert Pinkham Ryder, for example), discontented with inherited forms and willing to
traverse perilous netherworlds of experience in order to
reach total spiritual freedom.

This shadowy stream of American experience flowed
darkly and swiftly from 1900 to the end of the First World
War. In the twenties, at least in painting, the tide ebbed,
and when, in the thirties, the United States was overtaken
by the Depression, America drew somberly into herself.

To the painters the Depression meant an enforced respite from the struggle for spiritual liberation. The generation born before 1920 accepted the government's survival proposal, the Work Projects Administration, and not a few of the young painters were engulfed for a time by a painting attitude called "social realism." [3]

Many were stirred by the Mexican muralists Rivera, Siqueiros and Orozco, whose unquestioning commitment to social reform led them with enviable ease into the public arts. American painters who worked on the WPA's mural projects were caught up in the spirit and many of them tried to paint their humanist aspirations and social protest in overt idioms.

At the same time, the WPA brought painters together and they found themselves, for the first time in history, in what amounted to an organized community. Frequent conversations, exchange of impressions, arguments about avant-garde European versus American regionalist art ensued. New York painters who remember the host of dilemmas they faced in their art in the days of the Project point out that during the whole period, there were exhibitions of European abstract and surrealist painting in New York, and that such painters as de Kooning, Gorky, Pollock, Davis and Tworkov constantly debated the merits of an art free from expository and social reformatory intentions. What is more, many of the easel painters were developing fresh ideas in their own work (for some, the Project provided the first opportunity in their lives to work uninterruptedly on their painting) that had nothing to do with the prevailing social realism. The social realist spirit in painting never really enlisted their enthusiasm although theories of social progress did. It did, however, dam up intense emotions so that when the inevitable break occurred, it was devastating and total.

Feelings surged to a climax around 1940, and the cry for a fresh beginning, a break with both American social realism and traditions imported from Europe, sounded in identical terms that it had sounded in 1912. It was the recurrent American cry for liberation.

The most important single factor playing into the rejuvenescence of the avant-garde spirit after the Second World War was that many of the painters had quite simply come of age. A man born in 1905 was thirty-five years old when the war began. He was ready to look beyond the formulas of his apprentice years. The war provided a violent impetus. Painters were alert to the dangers of provincial isolationism. Something that transcended their own biographies and national history had to be created.

As before, in the days of *Camera Work,* Europeans helped to stimulate American reactions, or to provoke them. The war brought a number of famous Europeans to New York. Fernand Léger and Piet Mondrian may not have had a stunning personal influence on the painters, but their presence alone brought Americans that much closer to the realization of their own potential. The war also brought an extremely lively corps of surrealists, including André Breton himself. More militant than most, the surrealists lost no time in organizing exhibitions, publishing manifestoes and acquainting American painters with the abundant high spirits that had propelled their European movement. American painters hastened to relieve themselves of the literary burdens they had assumed during the Depression. Surrealism's homage to the psyche was the very agent needed to release emotions partially blocked by the language of social realism.

Each painter naturally chose his means from among the many alternatives provided by this renewed aesthetic freedom. An eruptive, inherently romantic temperament such as Jackson Pollock's sought relief in the use of symbol. He was early impressed by the most expressionist phases of Picasso, which he heightened with his own baroque line. Then he reached for psychological symbol, the dream hybrids of Miró, Ernst, Masson. To this he added his own schema of primitive and American Indian symbology. He, Mark Rothko, Clyfford Still, Adolph Gottlieb and others watched European modes and incorporated them in their own work, adding a vigorous, at times gross flourish. They finished by transforming their "content" altogether.

Theirs was a mood of rejection that colored even their public pronouncements. In 1940, the newly formed Federation of Modern Painters and Sculptors felt obliged to state: "We condemn artistic nationalism which negates the world tradition of art at the base of modern art movements." Three years later, in June 1943, after a hostile press response to the Federation's annual exhibition, Adolph Gottlieb and Mark Rothko wrote a much-quoted letter to the *New York Times* in which they spoke for the abstract artists. Their letter can be taken as characteristic for the time.

"Since art is timeless, the significant rendition of a symbol, no matter how archaic, has as full validity today as the archaic symbol had then . . . No possible set of notes can explain our paintings. Their explanation must come out of a consummated experience between picture and on-looker."

Adding that their pictures demonstrate their aesthetic beliefs, Gottlieb and Rothko listed a few:

(1) To us art is an adventure into an unknown world, which can be explored only by those willing to take the risks.

(2) This world of the imagination is fancy-free and vio-lently opposed to common sense.

(3) It is our function as artists to make the spectator see the world our way, not his way.

(4) We favor the simple expression of the complex thought. We are for the large shape because it has the im-pact of the unequivocal. We wish to reassert the picture plane. We are for flat forms because they destroy illusion and reveal truth.

(5) It is a widely accepted notion among painters that it does not matter what one paints as long as it is well painted. This is the essence of academicism. There is no such thing as good painting about nothing. We assert that the subject is crucial and only that subject matter is valid which is tragic and timeless. That is why we profess spiritual kinship with primitive and archaic art.

Their engagement and anger came out fully in a last paragraph in which they attacked "interior decoration, pic-tures for the home, pictures for the mantelpiece, pictures of the American scene, social pictures, purity in art, prize-winning potboilers, the National Academy, the Whitney Academy, the Corn Belt Academy, buckeyes, trite tripe," and they added for good measure a big "etcetera."

Some of the men who took an aggressively antitraditional stance spoke in the impatient, transcendental idiom resembling that of the French nineteenth-century symbolist poets. Few among them, however, were familiar with French poetry. Their expressions surged from the deep sense of "place and locality" that Poe had had, and that Baudelaire had recognized.

Robert Motherwell, the one painter who did have a direct involvement with romantic poetry, was one of the youngest in the group now identified as abstract expressionist. His romanticism emerges clearly in his writings: "Abstract art is a true mysticism . . . or rather a series of mysticisms that grew up in historical circumstances that all mysticisms do, from the primary sense of gulf, an abyss, a void between one's lonely self and the world. Abstract art is an effort to close that void that modern men feel. . . ." [4]

Motherwell's unintentional paraphrase of Rimbaud is typical of the attitude among painters in the 1940's. Mysticism — a retreat from the finite and a bid for the infinite — appeared in the many myth paintings then being created. It was nourished by a community of spirit.

But soon, even esoteric myth was to be rejected. In the rising revolutionary fervor the American painter wanted to remove all documented tradition from his work. Consequently, around 1948, symbol and myth were abruptly turned out. Rothko spoke with distaste of the "obstacles" in modern painting, listing them as "memory, history or geometry which are swamps of generalization." [5] And Clyfford Still, who eventually became the solitary romantic par excellence, later declared: "We are now committed to an unqualified act, not illustrating outworn myths or contemporary alibis! . . . Demands for communication are both presumptuous and irrelevant." [6]

Conversations among the artists were frequent and a few were recorded. In 1950, dozens of abstract artists participated in a three-day, closed-session discussion summarizing the past two years' meetings of the informal artists' club.[7] Their subjects were characteristic of the period. A great deal of time was spent arguing about the role of geometry in painting, and the dominant attitude — that geometric form is inhibiting — was reflected by de Kooning's insistence that "geometric forms are not necessarily clear."

Awareness of European tradition and an irritation with its persistence lay behind many of the discussions. The problem of when a painting was "finished" was particularly irksome. The general opinion that European art was too "finished" led American artists to rationalize their own lack of finish. A positive value was placed on the "unfinished" look. Motherwell summed up their position by pointing out that the American abstract painter was involved in "process." Ibram Lassaw, an abstract sculptor, declared that "a work of art is a process started by the artist."

Another idea that recurred in discussions was that the artist was within his painting rather than outside and detached from it (de Kooning: "I'm always in the picture somewhere") — an idea that Pollock had quite literally acted out when he painted his canvases on the floor from all four sides, and incidentally, an idea that the Italian Futurists had already proposed.

Finally, one of the most important central ideas — that an abstract painting has a subject — was heatedly discussed both in public sessions at the artists' club, and in private conversations.

There was a duality in American painting evident not only in the artists' statements but in the most extreme essays between 1948 and the early 1950's. In fleeing from materialism, and from the inroads of a technique-conscious culture, the painters sought to *dematerialize their concepts,* to take them out of the realm of commonplace association. But paradoxically, in order to do this, they had to put an even greater emphasis on technique and materials. In the initial break, painting became virtually materialistic. That is, the *matter* itself became the content of the paintings. This was true particularly in Pollock's case. When at last he parted with symbolism, he invented a new *technique* in which the purpose was to make the material itself the expressive agent. Material versus ideal, idea versus technique were the dual factors.

Willem de Kooning reflected the duality differently. Like his friend Arshile Gorky, de Kooning had at one time been attracted to the tender manner in which Picasso portrayed his circus people. But de Kooning brought a startling admixture of tenderness and violence to the Picasso-inspired style of his earlier work. His sweet pink and pale green early paintings of women, for instance, were swept over by a hand which willed distortion and seemed to resent its own finesse. Later, that hand, always aware of tradition, was to lash out in an exasperated fury in an effort to free itself of classical restraints.

Pollock, de Kooning and a dozen other painters successfully wrested the attention of American connoisseurs from Europe. They had expressed in forceful terms what Melville had seen rooted in the American temperament, "the infinite cliffs and gulfs of human mystery and misery." They had beaten down the ghosts of Europe and the bourgeois demands of their own environment, and soared up in an apocalyptic outburst. They had swallowed cubism, surrealism, and a host of other "isms" whole and only a few discarded bones were left.

The result was that around 1950 there was a flurry of talk about a "New York School" and a "Pacific School." A little later, "abstract expressionism" began to be referred to as a movement. For a moment painters were even willing to accept the mantle of a "school" in their need to displace the idea of the "Paris School" in the minds of their public.

There was little basis for a movement or school but there *was* a concurrence of emotion and a solidarity of intention. The painters whose work was most iconoclastic had the greatest influence. Because Jackson Pollock dispensed with brushes in certain of his paintings, poured paint from cans and dripped it from sticks, and worked on the floor from all sides, his painting was considered "action painting," a term coined by Harold Rosenberg, meaning in its most simple definition painting in which the gesture, the act itself, is significant. De Kooning too was considered a "gesture" painter and the high-voltage, broad, scooping brush stroke he invented was adapted by many other painters.

They were determined to annihilate "taste" and shock habit-formed visions back to an instinctive threshold. They saw European painting as overelegant and degenerate and wished to suppress all traces of elegance in their own work. The mistrust of elegance was cultivated by American painters who saw in it a means of their liberation from convention. Goethe had also admonished the artist: "Do not let the effeminate doctrine of the modern beauty-monger make you too tender to enjoy significant rough-ness."

5 : Overtones of Existentialism

THE PAINTER, like a magnet, attracts ideas to himself, but they are not always "influences." At the time the American painters were feverishly engaged in forging a vital new concept of painting, ideas flew about like shuttlecocks, minds were susceptible. Yet not a single one of the noted painters now associated with the new American painting ever troubled to construe a working philosophy.

When Alfred Barr wrote a catalogue foreword for the New American Painting Exhibition in 1958 he mentioned two philosophic "echoes" in the painters' statements — Existentialism and Zen Buddhism.[1] Beyond the faint echoes, no philosophy could be positively stated as having affected these artists. Artists generally approach systems of thought obliquely. They are aware of ideas that are "in the air," as they put it. Existentialism and Zen were in the postwar air of both Europe and the United States. Painters and other intellectuals detached floating axioms to help them articulate what had already come about in their own ·thoughts and work.

"Of the seventeen painters in this exhibition," Barr wrote, "none speaks for the others any more than he paints for the others. In principle their individualism is as uncompromising as that of the religion of Kierkegaard whom they honor. For them, John Donne to the contrary, each man is an island."

Although it would be an exaggeration to insist on the role of Existentialism in this indigenous movement, it is important to bear in mind the extent of speculation during the late 1940's. The term Existentialism occurred frequently in discussions in the artists' club in which Existentialist diction — the terms "situation," "ambiguity" and "commitment" especially — was common. Everyone was reading Sartre and Camus. Intellectuals close to the painters, such as Harold Rosenberg and Clement Greenberg, were interested in the implications of Existentialism and stimulated conversations among the artists. Painters struggled to "explain" their motives and wrestled publicly with philosophical abstractions in the late 1940's.

But, like everything European that Americans appropriate, Existentialism was transformed. It became something peculiarly romantic that finally had little to do with the original. Even Barr's statement that the painters regard each man as an island — an observation based on painters' remarks — is debatable, since the very same painters also insisted on the existence of a "subject" in abstract painting.

It's true that they cherished their individualism, but without exception, they assumed that they could generalize from their own experience to the experiences of others. "I think we start from a subjective attitude which, in the process of our endeavour, becomes related to the world," said Barnett Newman.[2]

The subjective attitude of the American painters on the whole differed fundamentally from that of European Existentialists. On a superficial descriptive level, they coincided. The broadest vulgar descriptions of Sartre's Existentialism might be applied to the American movement. A deceptive argument would run like this: The American painters were, like the Existentialists, concerned with individualism; with challenging pure reason; with the role of dread, failure and death in existence; with the importance of personal commitment and individual acts. In the absence of comforting systems of thought, which, with the Existentialists, they had rejected, the American artists felt the forlornness, the despair and the absurdity of man's position in the universe. So far so good.

But what of Sartre's insistence that man is responsible for each of his acts and that passion is not self-justifying? The American painters' use of automatism alone rules out the Sartrian brand of Existentialism. And his pride in passion is unabated. Where Sartre speaks of transcendence as "self-surpassing," making it clear that when a man surpasses himself, he does so seeking his limits, and returns always to the concrete situation, he rejects the great abstract universals that held such an appeal for American artists. Existentialism in its French guise can never admit mysticism. In America, though, reductions of Existentialist tenets led to strange conclusions. If man surpasses himself, the American painter might say, he never knows where he will land. Therefore, it is quite all right to regard painting as a process, as Existentialists regard existence as a project, and still arrive somewhere in the infinite, in the realm of mysticism, leaving the "situation" behind.

The subjectivism of Americans and that of Europeans certainly has profound historical affinities, but divergences are equally profound. All that can be stated definitely is that while neither European nor American painters were adept in Existentialist philosophy, all sensitive men reacted to a set of circumstances that the Existentialist writers defined as a human crisis.

A French painter more than thirty years old when the Second World War ended was familiar with the extended world economic crisis that had occurred after the First World War. He had seen revolt, exasperation and negation in the arts in the between-war period. Then he witnessed Spain, Hitler, Munich, and war in 1939. Defeat. Occupation. The perilous struggle of the Resistance.

Through these harrowing experiences, the French artist became aware of a loss of common values, as Camus pointed out. He experienced constant alarm participating in a society where "human grief is no longer a scandal." He was concerned with a loss of moral values — not abstractly, but in direct reaction to gas ovens and torture chambers. He felt a cold solitude that he attributed to a breakdown of communication.

An American artist of the same age had experienced the

despair of the Depression. His own, or others', hunger made him directly conscious of human deprivation, and impelled him to take responsibility. Sharecroppers in the South, lynchings, starvation in slums, were realities that could not be evaded. The political attitudes that developed during this period, reflected in his painting, made him sensitive to the debacle in Spain.

Then came World War II. But in America, there were no occupation and no resistance, no comrades tortured by the Gestapo. Instead, America grew fat. No one can assess the burden of guilt that fell upon the sensitive in this paradox of prosperity.

Camus and Sartre, after all, *had* fought in the Resistance. Or, as they proudly declared, they had *chosen* to fight. Sartre maintained that man is free because he can always say no, and he had had the good fortune to prove his point by saying no to something grand-scale: the Nazis. After what they had witnessed, there could be no equivocation. Camus clearly stated that those who, like him, survived were lesser men because they had chosen to do less. For all that, the French, tempered by fire, were able to look universal guilt in the face and find some measure of moral stamina.

The real problem of the Existentialists was to find a means to confront outrages that staggered the mind. They wished to benefit humanly from them, to become pure and ethical men through confrontation. First they had to "know" the concrete. (The Existentialist tendency, even before the war, was considered a search for the concrete.) It was the manly decision to assess unpleasant, concrete

truths that took postwar Existentialism beyond the abstract speculation it had been in Heidegger's first works,
into the active realm of everyday ethics in France — at
least for a short time.

Circumstances were different in America and the spe-
cies of guilt was different. I use the word "guilt," but could
call it anxiety, care, awareness. Paradoxes mounted. There
was a "search for the concrete." Yet the search was embodied more and more in abstractions, for the concrete was
slipping away into the world of flux, the world envisioned
at the turn of the century.

European and American artists had had at least one experience in common: they had discovered the futility of
closed systems — whether of thought, of aesthetics or politics. As Barr said, they honored Kierkegaard — or at least,
the attitude of Kierkegaard as it was absorbed by their
time, in that they mistrusted the crowds, the bourgeoisie.
They had seen the bankruptcy of "school," of "styles," of
"isms" and, caught in the malaise of the 1940's, had been
thrust into the open seas of abstract speculation. They demanded to know the heady pleasures of making a choice,
even if it were only to say no.

If anything, the American painter was quicker to recognize futility. Perhaps the greater burden of his guilt sup-
plied this insight which has since proved so compelling
even to the ethics-minded Europeans. Sartre had said,
"What counts is the total commitment, and it is not by any
particular case or any particular action that you are committed altogether." In their melancholy situation American painters had sensed this too. In the late 1940's, when

they were not yet "personalities" assimilated by the crowd, they took energy from their total commitment — that is, their series of actions which had to do with saying no to the past and finding a new structure. It is no accident that Harold Rosenberg dubbed the avant-garde artists "action painters." [3] Their work was to be the virtual symbol of their individuality. Their "engagement" was not to effect changes in the human crisis by means of deed, as Sartre would have it, but by offering *themselves* — that is, their works — as the concrete evidence that the individual exists: in the face of horrors, of technocratic sterilization, of the lies of mass communication.

Even this courageous immolation has its ironies. Struggle as they might against the "crowd," the American painters have lived to see the crowd (or untruth as Kierkegaard puts it) accept them. Kierkegaard had warned that the communicator of truth can only be a single individual: "For it often happens that a man thinks that the crowd is untruth, but when it — the crowd — accepts his opinion *en masse,* everything is all right again. . . ." [4]

(Ironically, current painting as a protest against mass communication tends to imitate the very thing it is protesting, by dint of repetition; painting in series, personal publicity and an insatiable hunger for wide public recognition. Certainly the mosaic approach in modern painting, in which each man repeats his symbol so that the grammar of painting is made of this man who is a noun, this one who is an adjective, that one who is a verb, seems to insist on the disappearance of the individual. It tends to become a community enterprise.)

The American painters who had been troubled by a confusion of art and ideology during the Depression and the subsequent war quickly established an irreconcilable dualism after the war. In a spirit of disillusion with political action, they exacted a complete schism between art and what they called "politics." Unlike their French counterparts, they disavowed an attempt to see the ethical man in his total context. As usual, the word "politics" took on a pejorative meaning for Americans. Theirs was to be a flight toward transcendence of all petty "organized" human actions.

Nothing reveals the bitter dualism that permeated the American art world immediately after the war as clearly as the journal founded in 1947 by Harold Rosenberg and Robert Motherwell called *Possibilities*.[5] The magazine was to represent artists whose individual works supported their belief that "through conversion of energy something valid may come out, *whatever situation one is forced to begin with.*" Naturally, the two founders wrote, the "deadly political situation exerts an enormous pressure." But, they said, political commitment in our times means, logically, no art, no literature. "If one is to continue to paint or write as the political trap seems to close upon him he must perhaps have the extremest faith in sheer possibility. In his extremism he shows that he has recognized how drastic the political presence is."

In short, it was once again the American leap out of local and temporal vicissitudes into the romantic void where it seemed *possible* — barely possible — to exist. For this reason, the American adaptation of the existential attitude was closer to the abstract philosophizing of Heidegger and Jaspers than to the applied philosophies of the young postwar French Existentialists.

The degree of high-flown abstraction in Heidegger's existentialist essays is commensurate with the degree of abstraction in painting and prose of his time. Walter Kaufmann in his book on Existentialism says that Heidegger belongs to the contemporary revolt against representation:[6] "Even as modern prose and painting are no longer satisfied with the representation of events or things, Heidegger feels that the time has come for philosophy to break with what he calls representational thinking . . . What Heidegger proposes in place of representational thinking he calls *das andenkende Denken,* a thinking that recalls . . . We must try to call back what is forgotten. Being, not beings; not mere objects but that of which we are a part."

This abstract existentialist vision of the relationship of the individual to the universe relates to the vision of the contemporary painter. He easily recognizes himself in the existentialist framework in which the unit, the ONE, is the object of intense speculation. Since Kierkegaard, the "existentialist sensibility" has demanded recognition of *authentic* experience. The centered individual, beset with "care," experiences a necessity to understand his position in a twofold relationship: to the visible and to the moral worlds.

"There always arises in thinking man that which passes beyond everything he thinks," says Jaspers. It is the "passing beyond" with which the artist is concerned.

The American artist tended to pass beyond, well beyond, the concrete examples of the search for Being prof-
fered by French Existentialists. His allusion to the "authentic experience" takes him away from the realities of
Sartre's man who confronts experiences and keeps invent-
ing fresh means (choices) to see them through. The main
thing in "passing beyond" for the artist is to reach for an
ideal unity — something Sartre could never allow. In this
sense, the American painters came closer to Heidegger's
almost mystical "thinking that recalls." They did so in two
stages. First, in their earlier search for primordial or arche-
typal symbols which led them to exploit ancient and primitive art and classic myths; later, in the development of
intuitive paintings that depended on revelation and a dialectic relationship to the cosmos.

6 : The Use of Myth in the 1940's

THE FIRST STAGE of looking for authentic experience in primordial symbol and classic myth, of "seeking a significant rendition of a symbol no matter how archaic," as Rothko and Gottlieb wrote, became apparent during the 1940's. Pollock, Gorky, Still, Gottlieb, Stamos, Tomlin, Rothko, Baziotes — to name just a few — turned insistently back deep into the past of civilization, to exercise the thinking that recalls rather than represents. In this they revived the romantic spirit of the early twentieth-century avant-garde.

No doubt they responded in part to the drift of European painting. Before Americans borrowed motifs from Greek myths they had certainly known Picasso's resurrections of the myth of the Minotaur; Paul Klee's excavations for enduring mythic symbols; de Chirico's interpretations of classic myths; surrealists' horseplay with bizarre Greek legends. Americans, however, used ancient sources sparingly as though it were already preordained that they were to travel quickly beyond specific myth.

When Picasso illustrated the first issue of the surrealist magazine *Minotaur* in 1933, his virile image of the bull-man as the dark principle traveled with incredible speed to studios all over Europe and the United States. It was an impressive event. Picasso's passionate adaptation of an ancient myth in modern dress was a stimulating idea quickly seized upon by many young painters, among them Americans. Even so, the avant-garde American painter instinctively avoided illustration. Characteristically, the clarity of French adaptations of ancient myth roused their suspicions. They were after more obscure, more general meanings.

In many ways American painters have always come closer to understanding the transcendentalism of the expressionists, and, in an indirect way, of Paul Klee. Too little has been said of Klee's influence, though it permeates contemporary art. His work was first shown in New York in 1924 by the Société Anonyme, and then was little heeded until the late 1930's. But artists conversant with European art were aware of Klee's philosophic position.

Klee's early use of myth and parable was essentially illustration and he himself condemned it as "epigrammatic" rather than plastic. Later he clearly set himself the task of expressing the cosmic truths he faithfully believed existed, in terms of pure symbols. The cryptic graphic language of letters, arrows and abbreviated symbols he developed was intended to summarize his philosophic concern with good and evil, with "ethical stability."

"All art is a memory of age-old things, dark things, whose fragments live on in the artist," he wrote. His profoundly serious attempt to make a personal cosmology was much nearer to American ideals of the 1940's than the mythmaking of the French. His transcendentalism was tinged with the earnest, invincible need for faith that has been known in a more naïve sense in American art for more than two centuries.

"Symbols reassure the spirit that it need not depend exclusively on terrestrial experience . . . Art plays an unwitting game with the ultimate things and achieves them nevertheless." [1]

The direct stimulus for American experiments with myth and archaic imagery came from the surrealists whose presence was felt in America early in the game. Even the surrealists, though, were understood by American painters in quite another vein than intended. The surrealists played with juxtaposed shock-symbols, sometimes drawn from ancient myth, sometimes inspired by totemic and atavistic objects. They played. Wit and "epigrammatic" felicities were more important to the orthodox surrealists than the foundation of a cosmology. Not so for their American converts, who could never shake their uneasy belief that a painting must be more than a play on words and more than a juxtaposition of startling symbols. It is significant that the aspect of surrealist imagery that most interested American painters was metamorphosing form. The initial experiment with metamorphic symbols in the United States was to lead directly to abstraction. A form if it appears to be in an intermediate stage implies *time.* The idea that forms could shift and grow on a canvas, that time itself could be suggested by forms, eventually developed in American painting into the abstract expressionist notion of "all-over" space. The shift from surrealist metamorphosis to an abstract condensation of the idea is easily seen in Jackson Pollock's development.

In his early youth Pollock was already in search of mysterious key symbols. While he was in his twenties and even before his contact with the surrealists, his paintings showed evidence of the qualities that were to become the hallmarks of his style.

The basic quality was an insistent stress on the curving form — the womb or cocoon enclosure. Even in his late "drip" paintings this persistent instinct for circular enclosure exists. There is an urge to integrate all of the canvas with interwoven forms suggesting duration, to expand the primordial symbol of eternity (the arabesque to which Pollock always returned) literally into infinity.

Pollock was in his early thirties when he painted "Pasiphaë." A long horizontal canvas, it was filled with charging lines and energetic forms reflecting the expressionist urge which was then, in the early 1940's, becoming manifest in the work of several painters. Pasiphaë, who seems to be making love to the white bull, is set in an ovoid central shape bastioned on either end with vertical centurions and side-stitched with quasi-symbolic biomorphic shapes. The electric moment, on the verge of orgasm, is caught in a rhythmic yet jogging line — a characteristic carried over late in Pollock's nonobjective paintings.

"Pasiphaë," "Totem" and several paintings of the midforties show Pollock moving away from the explicitness of European symbology. The ambiguities implicit in Pollock's paintings are already well beyond the specific nature of Picasso's renditions of ancient myths. Pollock's use of organic forms takes on a new significance, as did Arshile Gorky's during the same period. What André Breton called Gorky's insistence on the "hybrid" form applies to Pollock too. These hybrid gut-like shapes are invested with a meaning, but a meaning that strains beyond verbal definition. They are deliberately nonillustrative, deliberately painted to suggest a wealth of associations having little to do with the expository details of the Pasiphaë myth.

When Pollock and other painters became obsessed with totemic images and "inward" forms, and when they began to be concerned with a "handwriting" and the signs of the psyche, that was the moment abstract expressionism began to take shape. In making hecatombs on the altar of the unconscious, the American painters were sober and respectful. They thought not so much in terms of how they could "use" the unconscious — as did the surrealists — as how they could portray themselves as spiritual wholes comprising ethical, conscious man and "original" man with his primordial unconscious.

Pollock had freely admitted his debt to the surrealists. From them he took the courage to throw out overt image and find the symbols deeply embedded in his own tem-

JACKSON POLLOCK, *Totem II, 1945*. Oil, 72 x 60.

(*Collection of Lee Krasner Pollock, Springs, East Hampton, New York*)

perament in the act of automatic drawing. But it was not automatic drawing for its own sake: Pollock's end *was* to set in motion a thinking that recalls. His drawings of 1938 are spread out with equal emphasis on the surface, much as Masson's drawings. They were filled with familiar surrealists devices — vegetal shapes, distorted members of the human body, eyes and talismanic shapes. These drawings, however, were more a stage in Pollock's search than finished works in themselves.

If Pollock and the others were seeking basic human realities in a primordial, prelogical expression, they were not trying to resurrect *specific* myths. What they attempted was to invest their images with the aura of myth, the atmosphere of mysterious ritual. The disparate, floating signs and symbols were not to be interpreted as attached to a specific tradition, but simply to be seen as the cues to a mythic world not even the artist could accurately interpret. Their conception of myth was broad and vague, characteristically skipping over details to find the largest definition. Not a scholarly definition, but one coming close to Ernst Cassirer's: "The world of myth is a dramatic world — a world of actions, of forces, of conflicting powers. In every phenomenon of nature it sees the collision of these powers. Mythical perception is always impregnated with these emotional qualities." [2]

Myth is concerned with a vision of the unity of life, and in their divergent ways, the American painters were attempting to restore the unity which seemed to have been fragmented by their predecessors.

Arshile Gorky was particularly sensitive to the messages

of the surrealists but he, more than the others, struggled
to make firm his deep sense of myth.[3] Many of his paintings and drawings in the 1940's were connected in his
mind with a lost childhood that took on mythic qualities. (Gorky's reputation for embroidering on his childhood memories runs true to form. Anthropologists have
shown that the *need* for myth always stimulates individual
myth-creators to fanciful generalization. Logical "truth" or
historical fact is irrelevant to the mythmaker.) Gorky's
youth in Armenia, the folklore, the legend and song that
enlivened his childhood became for him a source as deep,
as prelogical, as symbolic of conflicting, unnamed forces as
any art based on established classical myths.

In 1941, Gorky wrote a legend for his "Garden in Sochi"
that clearly showed the mythic coloration of his imagination. This rhapsodic legend deserves to be quoted, so well
does it illustrate that phase of his work:

About 194 feet away from our house on the road to the
spring, my father had a little garden with a few apple trees
which had retired from giving fruit. There was a ground
constantly in shade where grew incalculable amounts of wild
carrots, and porcupines had made their nests. There was a blue
rock half buried in the black earth with a few patches of
moss placed here and there like fallen clouds. But from where
came all the shadows in constant battle like lancers of Paolo
Uccello's painting? This garden was identified as the Garden
of Wish Fulfillment and often I had seen my mother and
other village women opening their bosoms and taking their
soft and dependent breasts in their hands to rub them on the
rock. Above all this stood an enormous tree all bleached under

ARSHILE GORKY, *Garden in Sochi*, 1941. Oil, 44¼ x 62¼.

(*The Museum of Modern Art, New York*)

the sun, the rain, the cold and deprived of leaves. This was
the Holy Tree. I myself don't know why this tree was holy but
I had witnessed many people, whoever did pass by, that would
tear voluntarily a strip of their clothes and attach this to the
tree. Thus through many years of the same act, like a veritable
parade of banners under the pressure of wind all these personal inscriptions of signatures, very softly to my innocent ear
used to give echo on the sh-h-h-sh-h of silver leaves of the
poplars.

Gorky studiously kept his memories alive, injecting
them into the heart of his work. The sweet ache of nostalgia was the essence of his style.

When he was twenty-one years old, a poor art student,
he published a poem in English. It was awkward, in a
newly learned language, but true to his romantic temperament. "My soul listening to the death of twilight, kneeling
on the far-away soil of suffering, my soul is drinking the
wounds of twilight and of the ground; and within it feels
the raining dawn of tears . . ." The faraway soil of suffering and a raining dawn of tears remained Gorky's leit-
motifs until his death in 1948.

Born in a small village in Turkish Armenia, his first
nine years had been spent in a vivid Caucasian environment in which he rode his Arab horse high into the Ira-
nian mountains with the shepherds and learned their songs
and dances. The plaintive quality of those songs haunted
Gorky, whose own stories and poems had something about
them of the wild Caucasian lament.

Gorky's background, drenched with myth and folk tale,
provided him with innate resistance to the empiricism and

common sense of his new homeland. It taught him the advantages in turning back, away from the suffocating present, to a past in which the imagination could wander freely.

At first his turning back was prudent, leading him to study old masters along with established European modern masters. Picasso greatly inspired him. In 1926, Gorky, aged twenty-one, began a portrait of himself with his mother, based on an old photograph. Picasso's rose-period portraits had influenced his vision, but his own idiosyncrasies were already noticeable. The motif in itself — a grave image of an old-world relationship — was typical of Gorky and his incessant returns to an idealized past.

Picasso continued to exercise a strong influence on him, even after he was familiar with surrealism and neoplasticism. Gorky seemed to be determined to check his romantic impulses by imposing on himself the disciplines of cubism. During the 1930's, when many avant-garde American painters hesitated between the rigors of cubist composition and a less confining, free-form abstraction, Gorky epitomized the conflict in his remarks on Stuart Davis's paintings, which, he wrote, "move us to the cool and intellectual world where all human emotions are disciplined upon rectangular proportions. Here these relations take us to the scientific world where dreams evaporate and logic plays its greatest victory . . ." [4]

A place where dreams evaporate and logic triumphs could not, however, accommodate the turbulence in Gorky's soul. After wrestling with cubism for years and mastering the style, Gorky had to leave it behind.

Toward the late 1930's Picasso's influence yielded to that of Miró. When he entered the abstract space of Miró, Gorky was at last free to release his own sense of imagined spaces and myth, and it was shortly after, in the "Garden in Sochi" series, that he came to terms with himself.

In both drawings and paintings, Gorky began to picture a space that knew no boundaries. By painting thin overlays of related tones he was able to suggest trembling waves of atmosphere that echoed back into an illusory dreamworld that was his proper element. All the anatomical, biological, curving and erotic forms that obsessed him were laid out in disjointed sequences, drawn with a rare, fine hand that recalled the finesse of Paul Klee.

The jubilant sense of freedom Gorky experienced when he left behind the constrictions of cubism is conveyed in "Waterfall," painted in 1942, in which the cascade of forms, recalling the "raining dawn of tears" in his boyhood poem, flows unimpeded. Rills of paint trickle downward, line is used sparingly to indicate movement. The erotic shapes so important to Gorky — heart, testicle, liver, breast and buttock forms — are at the summit of the composition where Gorky believed eroticism belonged.

To these fragmentary forms, undoubtedly first suggested to him by the surrealists, Gorky added directly observed naturalistic details shortly after. Moving into his maturity, he compiled his world with increasing assurance, using the ambiguous diffusive space that he had created.

His last paintings revealed Gorky's great sensibility to color and light as well as his sensuous lyricism. In them, forms have a double life: they float in a mythical atmos-

ARSHILE GORKY, *Waterfall*, c. 1943. Oil, 60½ x 44½.

(*Sidney Janis Gallery, New York*)

phere, sometimes the atmosphere of splendid eastern sunlight, and they are fixed forever in it. The interrupted, hesitant character of line and tone he had cultivated slightly earlier is supplanted by firm composition. His work became more subtle, more abstract. The specific aspects of myth were generalized, as in "Untitled" (see frontispiece) where he unifies the surface, pushing the drama back, putting a veil between spectator and image as the mythical "aura" requires. The fragmentary forms lie beneath, still suggestive but generalized. A small rectangular inset, like a magician's treasure chest, contains hints of events — unspecified, mysterious events. He had, in these last paintings, gone beyond specific myth.

Gorky was ultimately concerned with what used to be called the "grand themes." All reference to biomorphic forms, to movement, to depth, finally was set within a framework of speculation on the very sources of life and death, of existence and being.

William Baziotes, who said that his paintings were his "mirrors," was haunted too by the distant-source imagery that makes a mythos. His paintings in the mid-1940's almost always included a veiled sun or a moon, or forms refracted by moonlight. Eyes, too, filled his mirrors, embedded in depth, with ambiguous light intended to suggest great distance — spatial and temporal — in his paintings. Sometimes he painted a known myth, as in "Cyclops," but more often fragments with unspoken mythical significance.

It was an easy transition for Baziotes later to go even further back, to the very sources, in his shimmering aquatic

WILLIAM BAZIOTES, *Cyclops,* 1947. Oil, 48 x 40.

(*Courtesy of the Art Institute of Chicago*)

pictures where the sea is unmistakably present, and the
forms within it protoplasmic.

Adolph Gottlieb, who along with Rothko had declared
his kinship with primitive and archaic art, painted a series
in the mid-1940's which were known as pictographs. As if
incised on clay, his symbols — often identifiably fish, eyes,
suns and arrows — were laid out in adjacent compart-
ments. Gottlieb was interested in specific symbol in cursive
paintings. His references to the established symbols appearing in primitive art were almost always direct.

Gottlieb's clearly defined pictographic paintings were
very similar to those of Joaquín Torres García, the Uru-
guayan painter. Although Gottlieb had never come into
contact with Torres García, and apparently had not known
his paintings, the convergence of the two is striking.

In 1932 Torres García published a small folio, *Reason
and Nature,* in which he declared: "We must return to the
great line — which finds its origin in prehistory." He
urged painters to search for the unity which is "the base of
thought and the base of ourselves." A letter, or a sign, en-
graved on a piece of stone, he explained, was something
that truly detached itself from nature. "It is the sign of
Man, the imprint of Reason."

This attempt to reconcile prelogical intuitions with reason — or unity — was made by Gottlieb, too, when he
clung to the symbol that was to express a "subject." Even
when he later altered his forms, made them cryptic, they always had the air of the symbol, of alphabetic sequence.

Gottlieb's paintings of the late 1950's are entirely con-
sequent. In them he reduced himself to one general motif,

ADOLPH GOTTLIEB, *Voyager's Return*, 1946.
Oil. 37⅞ x 29⅞.

(The Museum of Modern Art, New York)

JOAQUÍN TORRES-GARCÍA,
Arte Universale, 1938. Oil, 17 x 32.

(Rose Fried Gallery, New York)

interpreted by some as symbolic of atomic explosion, but probably a pictorialization of the general "cosmic" theme many artists pursue. In this single image Gottlieb faithfully reduced himself to the following: an abstract background for a composition divided by two forms against that background. Above, a flattened sphere, below, a ragged, mildly explosive form. Or variations thereof.

Although these are purist reductions, Gottlieb's tendency toward symbols urges him to invest them with literal associations. There is an inevitable earth-sky relationship and a naturalistic balance between the two. The scale of the "cosmic" reverie is immediately cut down by the easily reconciled balance.

Repeating his final sign reductions, Gottlieb forfeits the symbolic impact. Even such large themes as he seems to be approaching become trivial when reduced to alphabetic regularity. Here are the A, B, C in their pure form. But each is equal, each sequent. No summary sentence ever seems formed.

In many ways, Bradley Walker Tomlin's abstractions, drawn from an earlier concern with signs and symbols, also fail in the same way. By weaving his pictographic forms interminably, Tomlin moved from the charged atmosphere of promised significance — the mysterious message that seemed implicit in the signs — to a discreet aesthetic patterning. His consummate craftsmanship redeemed him on the whole, but he never quite succeeded in restoring the tensions necessary to make his art a "subject" art, which he, like the others at that time, deemed so important.

Mark Rothko's stated interest in the transcendental, in

creating a mythos, was carried out in his paintings of the middle 1940's. Pale evanescent tones described a world filtered through dreams. Curving fragments of forms, sometimes liver-shaped or heart-shaped like auguries, floated in this world that was faint, faint as the last echoes of a horn note. He seemed to be looking to a far-distant point to pick out the keys of his drama. Frequently, these paintings were divided off by horizontal striations, like levels of time, or perhaps like the floor of the sea confronting the ceilings of heaven. Later, even the symbols were to disappear, and only the "levels," the horizontal entities, were to be left.

In 1947, in *Possibilities,* Rothko had written about the archaic artists whose society accepted the transcendental monsters they painted. "But with us," he said, "the disguise must be complete. The familiar identity of things has to be pulverized in order to destroy the finite association with which our society increasingly enshrouds every aspect of our environment." In writing on "shapes" Rothko confirmed what he and Gottlieb had said earlier in their letter: "They have no direct association with any particular visible experience, but in them one recognizes the principle and passion of organisms." Here again is the American impatience with finite associations, the need to vault the boundaries of conventional myth-painting and suggest instead a vague but overwhelming aura of myth.

Clyfford Still, who was soon to break entirely with what he called "subject matter," was also concerned in the mid-forties with symbolizing dark "forces" in a mythic way. His painting evolved from symbols that were predatory,

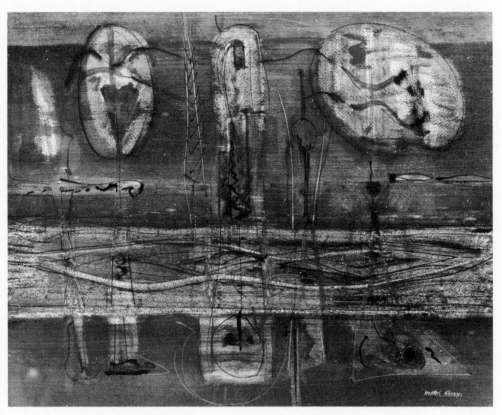

MARK ROTHKO, *Entombment I*, 1946. Gouache, 20⅜ x 25¾.

(*The Whitney Museum of American Art, New York*)

saturated with references to immolation, sacrifice and sexual ritual.

Without mentioning all the artists who in the 1940's went through this first stage of a thinking that recalls in terms of myth, it is apparent that in the United States, the return to myth and archaic symbol was one of the many means painters used to excavate their own psyches. Myth for them was not intended to suggest a meaning apparent to the community. Rather, it was a means of experiencing history and time personally and taking from the experience the material that seemed to illuminate the painter's individuality.

For this reason it was inevitable that most of these painters would make a rapid transition to an abstraction that dispensed with obvious symbol. Terrestrial experience was not enough. American painters, as recklessly drawn by the unknown as their romantic forebears, could not abide the limitations imposed by a mode that required definition and translation. They hungered for the infinite.

7 : Myth Transcended

WHAT I HAVE called the second stage in which intuition, or revelation, takes precedence over symbolic myth was reached in the late 1940's by many of the painters I have mentioned. Increasingly the painter saw himself as a "medium" with nothing intervening between him and his intuitive experiences. He offered himself, his work, as the irreducible evidence that the individual exists. He moved from the recall of ancient symbols to revelation. Instead of standing outside of time, memory and myth, he plunged unself-consciously into a quest for direct experience of invisible "forces." His broad generalizations were about time, space, titanic clashes of forces, the fragile tracery of man's presence. It was a lyrical romanticism staking everything on revelation, much as it was postulated in the days of Stieglitz's circle when "cosmism" was a key phrase.

In this introspective transcendentalism there is a distinct American flavor recognized by many Europeans who have approached American painting thoughtfully. French art historian Henri Focillon suggested the "locality" and character of American infinity-longing when he wrote in 1930:

"The American pioneer is not incarcerated in an island: he goes, he displaces himself, his taste is to live in the distance, to change, to invent himself. This is a majestic basis for an art . . . In the sites of the New World a vast soul can spread itself out, dilate itself at its ease without ever finding its limit." [1]

When open-minded European art critics saw the New American Painting Exhibition in 1958-1959, nearly all of them remarked on the introspective tendency of American painters. A large number of the written commentaries on the show included references to Poe, Melville and Whitman, in whom critics sensed the same desperate inward turning and supreme consciousness of unnamable forces as exists in these painters.

The critics who turned back to Melville were justified. Melville's peculiar mysticism that led him to dedicate a book to a mountain and to speak of "delicious poetic presentiments" lingers in America today. Melville longed to thrust beyond the boundaries of his vision and suffered constant melancholy defeat. "Deprived of Joy I find cause for deadly feuds with things invisible." His wonder and despair of the human condition persists in present-day romantic artists: "Far as we blind moles can see, man's life seems but an acting on mysterious hints." Hidden in this phrase are the intuitional, mediumist principles which project the notion that art is a way of probing for answers to the riddle of the cosmos — the view of art that still dominates American painting.

Whitman also provided Europeans with parallels. During his life Whitman, like Poe, had been lauded in Europe — particularly in England — while Americans turned away from him. He was appreciated in Europe for many of the same reasons Pollock is today. In his own time Whitman's work was described by an English critic as "symphonic" — the very term Clement Greenberg used to describe Pollock's abstractions. Whitman was admired for the way he sprawled and rambled in an emotional way no European, because of his culture, would have dared. He was understood to embody a typical American unwillingness to accept limitations.

To go beyond limits was the urge motivating most of the painters I have mentioned so far. Introspection, reliance on intuition became the rule, toward the 1950's. This second stage is well represented by Philip Guston. His questioning existentialist attitude (in the sense of self-surpassing) is described in his abstractions — physical symbols of his own relentless probing for the essence or definition of interior life. Not his own life only, but life itself.

The process by which Guston debates — taking both sides in an unending drama — could be called a cosmic dialectic. Now he is a concrete man, part of the natural world that is animal, vegetable, mineral. Now he is disembodied man, a mind in the unlimited seas of history — his own and the world's — attaching itself to ideas, fleeing them, battling with what he *knows* to exist but cannot see or touch. In whatever he undertakes to argue, both the "real" and the imagined worlds are present, and they are symbolized in the hope that the desired unity of existence may at one time or another be revealed.

In his own way Guston also worked through the first stage of myth, only his was a romantic rather than abstract approach in which fragments of real life — not abstract, ritual or symbolic objects — were woven into compositions suggesting myth. The difference between Guston's romantic first stage and Rothko's is like the difference between James Joyce, whose mythical allusions were comprehensive and integral, and Dostoevsky, whose mythical content emerges indirectly in essentially "realistic" novels.

Guston's figurative paintings were always complex reflections on the human condition. His major paintings before 1947 were usually static symbolic dramas. He painted cities in which endless rows of blind windows and spires, porch-posts and finials, suggested confinement, prison. He painted children, sometimes engaged in mock battles with wooden swords and paper hats, sometimes unnaturally quiet, staring far out of the life around them. There was usually one masklike innocent face, a symbol of lost innocence, the embattled individual in the midst of senseless chaos. The props Guston accumulated in his earlier paintings always seemed to be symbols of meaningless worldly clutter.

Orpheus, Icarus, Ulysses — perhaps these specific myths could be used to interpret Guston's figurative paintings. But more ligely, Guston, who was away from New York during the 1940's, was developing his images (as the painters in New York who were developing dream symbols) from a source that was intentionally ambiguous. His endeavor was to define some tragic essence in existence.

It was natural, then, for him to move into a genre of abstract painting in which the search is for essences. That is, for the great abstractions that have lived since the beginning of history in man's imagination and that are no closer to definition than they ever were. Guston is attempting to make visual analogues. These abstractions of love, hate, anxiety, calm, joy, despair are no longer conceived as translations of what he sees and feels, but as the conditions in themselves. By this inevitable short-circuiting of his process, Guston moved, after 1947, into the identical area of intuition and revelation occupied by the painters I have already discussed.

Guston's meditations in painting have always reflected his dialectic temperament. Like a pendulum, he has swung from equilibrium to disruption — sometimes stressing the one, sometimes the other, sometimes synthesizing them in a single image.

His earliest abstractions were harsh, depthless surfaces with linear tracery echoing old symbols — crosses and prisons and ritual musical instruments. They were dark and troubled paintings.

From these, he went into a silvery, calligraphic abstraction in which the canvas became light itself, and the linear strokes became restless agents seeking equilibrium. Evanescent and slipping into air, these paintings represent one pole in Guston's imagination: the atmospheric infinity in which the movements of ambiguous forms (lines) are analogous to the movements Guston knows to exist in nature, or the cosmos, but which are not visible.

Between 1953 and 1956, approximately, Guston moved away from linear lightness. His need to be in touch with the material, concrete world was answered by an increasing accent on the vital, material properties of the paint itself. Although in the series of pink-hued paintings Guston characterized phenomena of flux — water, clouds, light extensions — there was power accumulating beneath the tender small strokes. In the massing of his small strokes, Guston's chief image was that of diffuse, floating sensation. But gradually, the diffuse masses gave way to specific thickening of line, and these lines began to surge energetically to an implied crest. "Beggars' Joys" shows how the nuanced, beautifully shimmering atmosphere Guston had created became the setting for a focused drama.

In these paintings Guston juxtaposed form (lines or strokes) and unform (vaporizing tonal extensions). He was painting then, and ever since, portraits of an inner life. Building his surface slowly, almost classically, with underpainting, his canvases were heavy with transmigrations of forms.

Around 1958, Guston made a definite statement of the tension between his two principal means: the linear which had become mass, and the atmospheric. Using rougher textures, more active and more equivocal shapes, Guston carried on a dialogue within his paintings that was more compelling, more "tragic" in tone than anything that had gone before. The massed strokes were attacked by atmosphere which worried their edges and intruded in unexpected

PHILIP GUSTON, *Beggars' Joys,* 1954-1955. Oil, 72 x 68.

(Collection of Mr. and Mrs. Boris Leavitt)

places. Twitching, surging lines were countermanded by thin, neutral washes. Although there were some powerful notes in greens, oranges and blues, the grayed surroundings almost drained them. These heavy seas of atmosphere began to have a formidable weight, threatening to absorb everything.

Disquiet and even despair find their expression in the turbulence of these seas of wash and the agitation of queer forms that never seem to find their balance. These wildly disconcerted entities are direct projections of a troubled spirit.

Strange as Guston's recent images are, they are not cut off from the past. They carry within them reminders of original experiences. Guston intentionally uses the means he inherited from Western tradition. He does not disdain oil paint. He does not forbid himself the use of depth. He even avails himself of traditional perspective when his image demands it. When he paints a dense form it is a thinglike form built with the same materials and techniques that Rembrandt used. Even the cold blue and gray elements that pitch against the "thing" can be conceived of as remembrances, perhaps of Tintoretto's fantastical atmospheric storms.

What is original and important about Guston's painting is not the means he uses, which are incidental, but precisely, his image of a state of being.

Guston is capable of revisiting tradition without sacrificing a vision of present and future. When he paints animalesque shapes that appear to devour each other, they suggest a Dantesque, lightless underworld. But they also pitch forward, into a dreaded premonition of our own world to come. When he shows a "structure" reminiscent of a trellised gazebo, as he does in "Close-Up III," it partakes of many characters. In its floating aspect, with glimpses of light and air between its parts, it comes from a romantic heritage quite as beautiful as an Embarkation to Cythera. But again, in its floating, its instability, stressed by a horizontal bar of orange beneath it, it is a disturbing image of levitation.

Guston's paintings must be seen in their details. Much of the dramatic and rich emotional effect resides in the spaces between forms that open back into other spaces. The small dense areas of paint Guston often uses to prop up larger configurations (like the orange bar in "Close-Up III") are cues to the internal image. One flare of rust-orange beneath a dusky gray structure can tell a great deal about the emotional climate of a Guston painting.

The limits Guston strives to surpass are those of his own personality. They can only be defined by the continuing act of painting. His transcendentalism never lures him away from the changing temporal events within his own experience.

Mark Rothko, on the other hand, differs from Guston or Gorky in that his spirit of transcendentalism wafts him away from the seething world of shifting details to which the other two painters temperamentally belong. He had spoken about pulverizing the familiar identity of things, of transcending the "finite associations with which our society enshrouds every aspect of our environment." He was one of the first to banish thinglike or mythlike symbols

PHILIP GUSTON, *Close-Up III,* 1961. Oil, 70 x 72.

(Collection of Lee V. Eastman)

from his paintings. He has minimized reference to the daily minutiae of experience in a monumental effort to reach exalted summary. He makes the romantic assumption that his aesthetic revelation can be generalized as a statement of human experience.

In his way he is always speaking of *la condition humaine.* He too is articulating through his humanity, through his amplitude of emotion and intuition, the highest points of human experience. He speaks in the various voices of pain, joy, perplexity, but always in extreme metaphor. He has no patience with transient phenomena but wants to go beyond the effect of many small sense impressions to a world of idealized universals.

If Rothko became a transcendentalist around 1950, when he dispensed with small detail and evolved the simple, spacious, rectangular image, he did not become a blind absolutist. He understands that an absolute cannot express his full humanity. No matter how abstract, he will always find a finite measure. He will use a concrete noun or a familiar verb to lead us into the vastness, into the greater reality of the poem. There are both abstract and concrete elements in any major work of art. Take Shakespeare's Sonnet LXV:

> *Since brass, nor stone, nor earth, nor boundless sea,*
> *But sad mortality o'ersways their power,*
> *How with this rage shall beauty hold a plea,*
> *Whose action is no stronger than a flower?* . . .

Vastness (boundless sea) is made conceivable through the solidity of nouns (brass, stone). And beauty, a transcending abstraction, is made conceivable through the fragile image of the flower.

Rothko, in painter's terms, does the same. It is through his zones of ambiguity — those shivering bars of light between major forms — that Rothko can move us. Through these tremulous passages creep our finite but infinitely nuanced emotions, finding their expression.

Within the strictly enforced limitations Rothko set for himself, he found the means to define certain universal responses to existence.

Although after 1948 he was no longer interested in the "principle and passion of organisms," he was still interested in the "subject" in his paintings. And it is, in his own view, a "tragic" subject that he is painting. In 1956-1957 Rothko's paintings were for the most part in clear, high-keyed colors, with much deep-dyed red and sun yellow. One painting of that period, for instance, was enormous, horizontal, with a field of yellow bordered by red edges. By its scale alone it verged on the proportions of epic drama. Since the eye must travel through the great desert of seemingly limitless yellow before it hits obstruction (and at that, a nearly illusory obstruction because of the fading edges), the experience cannot be immediate, or of a piece. The very time it takes to reach a visual resting point while regarding the picture creates anxiety.

Rothko's exhibition in 1958 showed him in a different mood (a mood he has sustained since) although the same rectangular scheme prevailed. With overwhelming prescience, the large, resounding paintings embodied Rothko's ineffable sense of tragedy. There can be no doubt that his

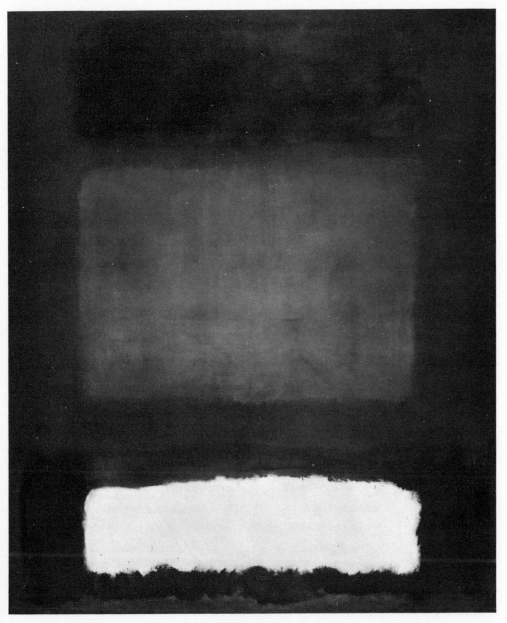

MARK ROTHKO, *Red, White & Brown*, 1957. Oil, 99½ x 81½.

(Kunstmuseum, Basel. Courtesy of Sidney Janis Gallery, New York)

colors, intuitively selected I'm sure, are symbolic. His blacks, which are never blacks but masses of deep, rich hues, are intended to express forbidding, wracking emotion. His purples, thinly layered and with great depths, are more melancholy than the most melancholy ruminations of figurative painters. When, through the interstices of these deep, minor-keyed compositions, a glimpse of pale light is seen, it is as moving as the light of distant paradise in a naïve early Renaissance painting.

There are Existentialist echoes in Rothko's words and in his attitude toward his own works. Yet I think that Rothko is characteristically American in his adaptation of Existentialism. He arrives at what appears to be its opposite in his work. Rothko's impatience with anything that is intermediary, with all that he considers equivocal and therefore half-lies in painting, has led him to remove nearly everything known from his paintings and to enlarge his format to extraordinary proportions. This sweeping renunciation he regards as a "unique act."

He has publicly discussed Kierkegaard's notion of "the unique act which society cannot condone," and has said that he is concerned with the relationship, or oppositions, of what he considers "universal law" and "individual law." [2] Moreover, he has repeatedly stated that he is a materialist and wants no part of the "otherworldly" interpretations of his work.

As existentialist in tone as Rothko's public statements are, his works remain transcendent symbols. Unlike the Existentialist, he does not feel compelled to invent a choice at each moment. He has worked out a greater scheme (his series of very similar compositions) within which he alters his drama according to his mood. "Small pictures are like tales," he has said. "Large pictures are like dramas."

The impressiveness of Rothko's large pictures is hard to convey, for they have never been seen in the context Rothko intended. A note in the Museum of Modern Art catalogue for his 1961 exhibition states simply that in 1958 he began a series of murals for "a large private dining room in New York." After eight months of work, "the artist decided they were not appropriate for the setting and therefore did not deliver the works."

These great enigmatic murals with their uncompromising simplicity bore with them a sacrosanct aura that no words of the artist can dispel. They were painted in a huge gymnasium that Rothko had converted into a cathedral-like studio. Seen there, in dim light, the paintings had presences as the murals in Renaissance stanze. To enter this studio was like walking into an old theater drenched with history, or a library permeated with the sense of flight and removal from hurly-burly events. Rothko had made a consecrated place for himself, and when some of the panels were subsequently removed from the "place" and exhibited out of context, they appeared strangely isolated.

Deep red, purple and black dominated in these murals. The solemnity of the colors stressed the iconlike simplicity of the rectangles they housed. Certain of the panels depicted long rectangular structures that seemed to be on the point of collapse, and could be read, as Rothko might say, as characters in a drama. Everything about these murals conspired to create an effect of hermetic symbolism that can only be likened to the effects achieved by frankly ecstatic mysticists.

Nevertheless, with all its inconsistencies, Rothko's concept of the "unique act" is perhaps the root of his style. For Rothko was one of the many painters who regarded "risk" as an essential part of his process, and who saw himself as a reactor, or fugitive from an uncongenial society. In his way, he was an "action painter" just as much as de Kooning or Kline if we accept Harold Rosenberg's 1952 definition of action painting already quoted: "At a certain moment, the canvas began to appear to one American after another as an arena in which to act."

Rothko's serious exasperation, acted on the huge area of his canvas, might be considered peculiarly American if only for his audacious decision to disregard historical precedent completely. His "act" is to register a fact so large in scale, so inundating as a sensuous object, that all questions of style and technique residing in tradition, even the modern tradition, are drowned in it. Perhaps this is why Rothko's painting has had such a powerful impact abroad.

Not all the breaks with the past tradition were as sharp as Rothko's. The atmosphere that bred discontent with inherited forms acted differently in the case of many other painters who were nevertheless committed to an idea of a "new" painting.

Robert Motherwell, one of the most complex personalities to come out of the avant-garde revolution of the 1940's, wove back and forth in time, space and tradition with tremendous agility. He too invokes the name of Kierkegaard frequently, but again, an innate romanticism keeps urging him beyond even the cultured references of his own past.

In 1954 he quoted Kierkegaard in a way that suggests his own credo: "If anything in the world can teach a man to venture, it is the ethical, which teaches to venture everything for nothing, to risk everything." [3]

It becomes increasingly apparent in Motherwell's work that venturesomeness, risk, flight to the unknown and experiment are the values he most cherishes. His development could be graphed in great swinging arcs that move in bewildering patterns through the history of modern French painting to expressionist painting to modern American painting and back again.

Motherwell is an extraordinary diarist who has offered a record of his intimate experiences freely in the course of his career. When he made collages in the 1940's, they alluded to his great affection for French culture. In the 1950's, they gave more complicated testimony, combining the impulsive, impatient techniques of abstract expressionism with the witty, orderly techniques of European collagists. Most recently, they are strange witnesses of a temperament that has leaped jubilantly into a world of sensation.

As a painter, Motherwell has undertaken many ventures. In the late 1940's, he often worked with a strong cubist impulse, painting large, clear planes in orderly sequences and simple forms. A natural elegance distinguished these paintings — an elegance Motherwell seemed bent on suppressing. Soon after, he covered his tracks in an emphatic leave-taking from cubism.

Motherwell's recent work is related to a long series of paintings commemorating the Spanish Republic. Nearly all of the elegiac versions in the early 1950's consisted of stark black, white and ocher schemes calculated to strike with funereal gravity. The symbolism, variously interpreted, remains general. Black verticals march mournfully across the surface, imprisoning oval forms between their bars. The black ovals have been choked into deformed shapes and hang helplessly between the verticals. In most versions, they are bound on either side by black borders.

From these elegies Motherwell went on to experiment with large monochrome shapes, developing the profiles, the wavery outlines, in order to express inner energies. Amorphousness itself is expressed.

Audacity is Motherwell's most admirable quality. If a retrospective exhibition were mounted now, while he is still a relatively young man as painters go, the extent of his willingness to "risk" everything would be amply demonstrated. His losses and weaknesses in the elaborate course of his painting evolution would be negligible when compared with his original experimentation.

James Brooks is another painter who moved from a cubist orientation into a personal, abstract expressionist idiom sometime in the late 1940's. His first important exhibition in 1950 included a number of silvery abstractions in which broad ribbons of subdued tones were woven into perpetually moving compositions. He experimented by painting on the back of his canvases and picking up the shadowy, suggestive forms, developing them on the front.

He described his method at the time as improvisation. "My purpose is to get as much unknown on the canvas as I can. Then I start digesting or changing. The first thing is

ROBERT MOTHERWELL, *Elegy to the Spanish Republic*, 1957-1961. Oil, 70 x 90¼.

(*The Museum of Modern Art, New York*)

to get a great many unfamiliar things on the surface."

The unfamiliar forms Brooks developed were insistently curving and suggested natural phenomena. Heaving rhythms characteristic in his paintings can easily symbolize the sea, or rushing waters, or sweeps of undulating landscape. Yet his work is essentially abstract, for he never begins with a subject in mind.

Brooks's recent paintings are bolder in color, and, instead of choppy linear sequences or elegantly curving strands of color, he has massed large areas of saturated red, blue, orange and green. Skillfully he leads the eye back into gleaming white spaces, or a dense blue-black horizon, illuminating its expanse by means of a few impulsive strokes of vivid color.

He still works on the principle of improvisation, striving to discover what he has called a mystery: the meaning within a painting that is more than merely the sum of its articulated elements.

Jack Tworkov, who had painstakingly perfected a delicate painting technique in early portraits and still lifes, moved only gradually into abstraction in the late 1940's. Of a meditative temperament, Tworkov had long pondered the history of art and was deeply steeped in mythology. "A painter is reliving all the things that Homer and Dante are about," he once said. He shared with Gorky a preoccupation with his childhood and for a long time sought to create a personal mythology based on the disparity between his well-ordered, old-world formation and his experience in the chaos of New York.

Eventually, like his New York colleagues, Tworkov con-

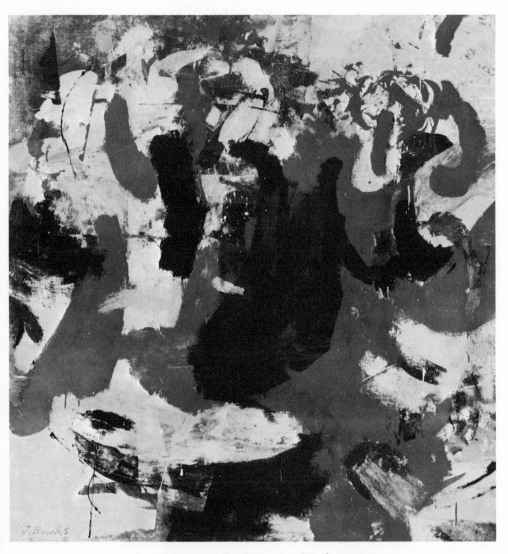

JAMES BROOKS, *Qualm*, 1954. Oil, 61 x 57⅛.

(*The Museum of Modern Art, New York*)

cluded that no past could reveal the truth he sought: "Above any esthetic view or the problem history imposes on us the thing is still to work closest to one's own Feeling," [4] he wrote. And, reflecting the existential sensibility, he added that an artist has to "find necessity, despite all confusions, deep in one's life, which happens to be, at bottom, everybody else's life too."

Tworkov's tendency is to veil the drama in his paintings; to thrust a grid or screen across his surfaces so that the events — often terrible events — are sensed rather than seen. His abstractions in the early 1950's were often smoothed over, with only a line here, a point there, reading through the pierced surface.

Gradually, Tworkov developed the feathering stroke, often diagonal, which is the peculiarity of his style. Within the blur and tremble of his brushwork, there are many suggestive shapes — sometimes figures, sometimes objects like bridges, trestles, cat's cradles. In Tworkov's case, a painting is certainly the sum of its destructions, for he goes over and over a painting, giving it a layered existence.

Tworkov's art is one of nuance and suggestion. He shares with his contemporaries a desire to go beyond what he knows with his eyes to a realm where the imagination is free to dream. The indeterminate appears in many of his paintings in the tapering mists of pale yellow, pink and white fading into infinity. Everything is blurred, as if seen through a glass: the metaphorical glass of time and history.

Sometimes his paintings carry with them a deep mystery that suggests his preoccupation with myth. "Blue Cradle," for instance, is woven and interwoven with varied hues of

JACK TWORKOV, *Duo I*, 1956. Oil, 81¾ x 57¾.

(The Whitney Museum of American Art, New York;
Gift of the Friends of the Whitney Museum of American Art)

blue with purple undertones. Evanescent horizons seep away from the blue edge, suggesting the light over heavy, deep seas, the cradle of life. Later paintings are even more circumspect, seeming to refer to the atmosphere of the sea, but in reality essentially abstract. Man is nowhere in these visions of infinity. He is merely able to imagine them, to be awed by them, to express them through the large, ceremonious canvases.

There were other painters who, like Tworkov, came only slowly, and after much troubled dialogue with their own pasts, to the second stage. A number of them had been born in Europe. I think of Esteban Vicente, whose collages and paintings are often considered related more to cubism and its later European variants than to the American post-war style. Notwithstanding his avowed classicism, his rejection of expressionist action and his fundamental antipathy for the Dionysiac strain in much of American painting, Vicente is an idealist who has assimilated introspective, intuitional principles in his work.

Although in Vicente's integral world of equilibrium there are no accidents, there are also no boundaries, no fixed spaces. What Vicente admired in the paintings of Juan Gris — the "profound stillness and gravity" — becomes, in his own paintings, a drifting stillness and gravity not held, as Gris's paintings were, within clearly defined limits.

During the late 1940's, Vicente painted refined, crisp abstractions that maintained the illusion of depth and suggested a profusion of indoor and landscape detail. By 1952 he had eliminated all but essential pictorial problems, us-

ing rectangular forms adapted from his superb collages.
Subsequently he readmitted curving and inconclusive
forms suggesting movement, but combined them with
large areas of tranquil color. In his most recent paintings,
there is unrest, calculatedly posed in the spreading quality
of the shapes.

Vicente's collages are remarkable. He has a unique way
of building an image from the ground up, adjusting and
superimposing his papers as he would with a brush. Or-
dinarily in a collage, the plane is "given." That is, the cut
paper is a flat surface applied to a flat surface. But in Vicente's collages, in which the papers are tinted with his
own hand, there are nuances and transitions — almost invisible — that provide an uninterrupted flow of forms
within space. Such fuguelike sequences are rare in the medium. Sometimes Vicente allows a carefully torn form to
hang free within his composition, thereby establishing a
complicated space: the immediate surface of the applied
paper; the space in between; the shadow that slides beneath
and the space created on the carrying ground-plane by
means of color. The tendency is to evoke a dreamlike suspension that softens, heightens and fuses shadowy elements
of feeling into a substance unknown before. Despite the
clarity of structure in Vicente's work, particularly his collages, there is a dreaming into the limitless spaces characteristic of the new American painting.

The painters I have discussed in this chapter represent
only a fraction of the community that found its voice after
the Second World War. Their most salient common bond
is a rejection — after greater or lesser struggles — of tradi-

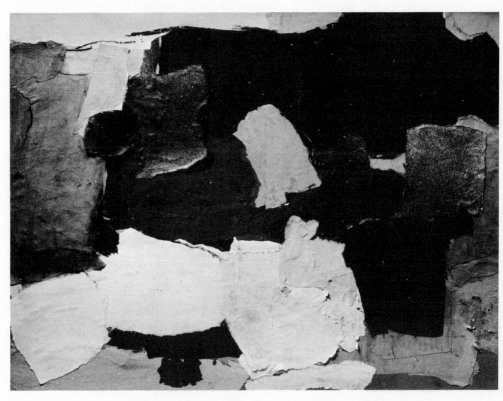

ESTEBAN VICENTE, *White, Black & Gray,* 1961. Collage, 27 x 36.

(*Dallas Museum for Fine Arts*)

tion as a basis for artistic development. They were without exception well versed in the development of modern and past painting history, had studied and developed in the Western tradition, had been influenced by European modern art. But liberation from conventions, all conventions (in itself a tradition they inherited from the American past), was the ideal.

8 : A Love-Hate Relationship to Western Tradition

No PAINTER better illustrates the American artist's struggle with an equivocal relationship to Western traditions than Willem de Kooning. In a sense, de Kooning is the purest embodiment of the existentialist attitude, for he has never submitted to "closed systems" of any kind. In his anarchic, Dionysiac way, and with his extraordinary store of vitality, he has run an obstacle course of his own making that defies charting. His openness to all experience, and therefore to his own incessant evolution as a painter, is responsible for the great influence he now exercises on American painting.

De Kooning more than anyone believed that "through a conversion of energy" valid work would have to appear. Unlike most artists of his generation, he had never given any sustained attention to organized institutions, be they

political, ethical or artistic. He had never tried to find unity
through the deliberate application of myth to his paintings.
The "obstacles" that he put in his own way were always
idiosyncratic, derived from intimate experiences. Paradoxically, his existentialist openness to other experiences
quickly displaced obstacles, so that de Kooning's life is a
continuously and radically modified monologue. If there is
permanence, it is in the residue of the deepest authentic experiences carried along in his paintings.

His is an art of incipient confession, checked always by
experience. If he finds his inspiration in the immediate
life around him, as he usually does, it is put to a thousand
tests — not consciously, but by authentic artist's reflex. Always lingering in de Kooning's consciousness are references
both backward and forward in time. His relationship to the
history of art is a troubled love story that can find no reso-
lution. "There is a train track in the history of art that goes
way back to Mesopotamia," he has said.[1]

De Kooning, in fact, puts himself into relationship with
the past by rejecting it over and over. Essentially, his is a
humanist attitude. "When I think of painting today," he
wrote, "I find myself always thinking of that part which is
connected with the Renaissance. It is the vulgarity and
fleshy part of it which seems to make it particularly Western."

He instinctively withdraws from Oriental art, or its
Western echoes in the work of the purists, because of the
very absence of vulgarity. The philosophic fixity Mondrian
sought is uncongenial to de Kooning. "The idea that nature is chaotic and that the artist puts order into it is a very

absurd point of view, I think. All that we can hope for is to put some order into ourselves."

At the same time, de Kooning is quite capable of admiring Mondrian, and of rediscovering some submerged aspect of himself in a style that previously alienated him. Perhaps the most telling public remark he ever made was when he said in 1951 that "some painters, including myself, do not care what chair they are sitting on. It does not even have to be a comfortable one. They are too nervous to find out where they ought to sit."

This nervousness, or openness, is salutary in de Kooning and the other artists he refers to. Experience may be fleeting but profound; it is undergone, forgotten, retrieved and re-experienced in the continuing agony of existence, just as it is for Giacometti, who once expressed the constant disquietude of the experiencing artist in a short description of his first trip to Venice. There he became enamored of Tintoretto, and nothing seemed to have ever meant anything to him but Tintoretto. One day, he went to see the Giotto murals, and he was stricken. Tintoretto, he reported, was also stricken with him. Suddenly, Tintoretto "became vague and floated away" while Giotto held him. That is, until he discovered Egyptian statuary. The Egyptians enthralled Giacometti for a time, until some other experience came his way. Finally, Giacometti ends his memoir with the sad confession that "all this has come apart these days. . . ." [2]

For de Kooning, too, things are always coming apart. But they leave their powerful residue which, milled by de Kooning's imagination, nourishes his art. Although "breaking up" and finding obstacles (which are virtually expressed in his painting) are natural processes for de Kooning, he too seeks an integrity, or unity, in his work. And it is through his drawing — he draws incessantly — that he has found the means, no matter how temporary, of expressing a personal alphabet that is not only orderly, but readable, despite the expressionist flourishes.

The peculiarities of de Kooning's line may be seen in the earlier somnambulistic portraits, particularly of women. He experimented with dislocations of perspective, placing, for instance, a pink plane partly behind a pale green plane, interrupting the lines of both, and suggesting a continuous space between them. In defining the features of his sitters, or imaginary sitters, he left hiatuses in the line, thereby creating other planes. This judicious interruption of line is the hallmark of a good draftsman and may be seen in any major draftsman from Leonardo to the present.

In always leaving an open area, whether in the color planes or the activating lines, de Kooning revealed a fundamentally baroque tendency later to be fully expressed in paintings such as "Attic" and "Excavation." Here, the line, weaving in and out of a shallow foreplane, is not calligraphic and abstract, as the line in a Pollock painting, but rather carries the memory of concrete objects — particularly human limbs — within their slightly shaded contours.

The demonic impulse that is never far from the surface in de Kooning's work, no matter how tender, occurs not only in these abstractions of the late 1940's, but in the famous "Woman" series that so startled the art world when it was exhibited in 1953. In these paintings the cubist

WILLEM DE KOONING, *Excavation*, 1950. Oil, 80⅛ x 100⅛.

(Courtesy of the Art Institute of Chicago and Mr. Edgar Kaufmann, Jr. and Mr. and Mrs. Noah Goldowsky)

method of taking fragments of reality, analyzing them, and putting them together again in startling contexts is combined with the expressionist's means. Like the expressionists, de Kooning often conceives of a painting as an analogue to observed nature.

The pitch of excitement in these portraits of vulgarity, these toothsome, fleshy women, misled many commentators into regarding them as descendants of the German expressionist earth goddesses.

In criticism of the show, the symbol of the prodigal artist returning to the great earth-mother was worked over thoroughly, although very shortly after the exhibition of the women, de Kooning was already exhibiting abstractions again. The last of the ladies in the series had metamorphosed sufficiently to make littérateurs think twice before invoking their Liliths, Medeas and assorted fertility goddesses!

It is commonplace to say that painting is concerned with relationships — of man to space, time and environment. But too often the critic fails to understand that while the quest for clarification of relationships never changes, the nature of an artist's information does. When de Kooning first painted the blowzy women, it was in keeping with his search for particular humanist principles. The fact that he implied environment through and within the woman's figure bears this out. In coping with the human figure, and later, with the figure in landscape or specific place, de Kooning extended his intelligence of the world and made forceful his intuitive knowledge of relationships. His way back to abstraction was not back at all. These paintings,

WILLEM DE KOONING, *Woman I*, 1950-1952. Oil, 75⅞ x 58.

(*The Museum of Modern Art, New York*)

like the abstractions that followed them, are the response of a vital, sensuous man to a complex of experiences — to the luxurious sensation of space, the rhythms of things in space, the magic of light in space and his own motor negotiation of space. And, above all, to woman, a being in space.

Shortly after he painted the "Woman" series, de Kooning shifted pictorial emphasis, suppressing his curvilinear impulse. He renounced chiaroscuro and sinuous line in order to experience the broad designations of space used by the painters who composed one flat area behind another in parallels. Such composing prohibits the curving flourish and rounded shapes. Since all growing or organic shapes have curved walls, the curve itself is a symbol for that which is living. In moving into flat forms and somewhat angular composing, de Kooning discovered a virtual abstract realm.

Even so, he could not down his baroque impulse entirely. The flat of his brush continued to pick up half-tones, twisting capriciously as it moved. At a time when he seemed to hunger for the detached experiences known by completely abstract artists, de Kooning could still not defy his own temperament, the baroque love for all that is incipiently mobile.

In one group of paintings, however, around 1959, he reached a passionately desired terminus. Although the canvases were distantly derived from landscape, they denied the existence of a middle ground and local color, and described an abstraction: vacancy.

The subject of the paintings was the void. In some of

them, void is like sky, painted bright blue; in others, void is like a channel leading out to sea, moving from one corner diagonally to the opposite corner. Still others showed void as the plane dropping off abruptly into ether. Whatever events occurred on a major plane were qualified by an open void.

The experience of vacancy is a basic human experience, occurring not only in reveries, but in waking physical life. In deliberately emptying his canvases, de Kooning evaded the clamoring willfulness of thinglike forms that reside in him.

In his most recent paintings, the sense of large, anonymous and alluring spaces persists. De Kooning's swinging brush swiftly marks out a series of horizontals. Just behind them is elusive infinity, either a dazzling pink infinity or a sparkling blue infinity. Canopies of denser color push back these nameless spaces. They are not to be attained and de Kooning accentuates their beautiful surfaces so that the loss of this paradise is keenly felt. Finally, color and the extremely personal imprint of de Kooning's rhythmic brush are the only bearers of association: flesh pink, sky and sea blue, sun yellow and grass green.

De Kooning had to know what abstract space based on the plane means. The straight line gives static poise. The curve, on the other hand, immediately penetrates space. By denying the curve in these pictures, de Kooning fulfilled a need that had been expressed periodically in his past.

Still, de Kooning's vivid impulse to the line which wings out and hooks into space is endemic, just as it was to Rembrandt, who also learned to curb the impulse by incorpo-

WILLEM DE KOONING, *Door to the River,* 1960. Oil, 80 x 70.

(*The Whitney Museum of American Art, New York; Gift of the Friends
of the Whitney Museum of American Art*)

rating broad horizontal and vertical planes in his later drawings. In Rembrandt, the baroque was opposed to a classicizing instinct, and I think the same may be said of de Kooning.

If we compare a detail of a Rembrandt drawing with one of de Kooning's sketches for the "Woman" series, the parallel is justified. Rembrandt's immediate impulse was to let the curving line of the wagon top arch out into space. The shafts or harnesses and bent rods holding the wheels repeat the vivacious hooking line. These impulsive hooks are also seen in de Kooning's drawing.

De Kooning's humanism, his intense preoccupation with the quick, the mobile, and its reception by the individual, always re-emerges. His "image" is a refraction of figures, landscapes, objects, all intensely experienced. The hooks, angles, sweeping curves, abrupt interruptions are hieroglyphs for the crook of an elbow, the bend of a knee, the stretch of a smile, the graffiti on sidewalks, cornices on city buildings, debris of city demolitions. His work is not a pastiche of stylizations. On the whole, de Kooning has avoided the trap of technocratic habit. He has not settled down to a "style" or to a particular image, but both style and particular image finally inhere in his work.

Like everyone else, he has had to make reductions, to scrape down his visions to their fundamentals. But since his rhetoric is elastic, and since he is not paralyzed by logic as a more systematic aesthetic thinker might be, he has remained a hardy receptor. He is not afraid to use the past — or in fact anything — to further his adventure in painting.

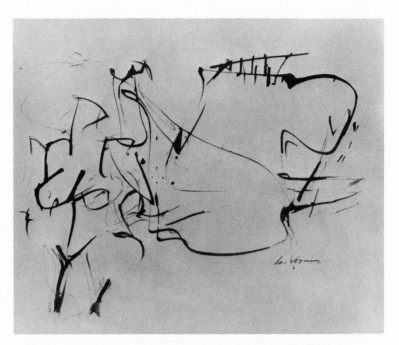

WILLEM DE KOONING, *Figure and Landscape,* 1954. Ink, 16 x 20.

(*Collection of Mrs. Martha Jackson*)

REMBRANDT VAN RIJN, *Village Street,* detail.
Pen heightened with white, 5¾ x 7½.

(*Collection unknown*)

Probably because of the latitude de Kooning has permitted himself, his influence on younger painters has been considerable. It has shown up particularly in two modes of painting that became prominent in the mid-fifties: expressionist figurative painting and neo-Dada collage.

The younger painters who resurrected the figure as a vessel for their observations on the human condition followed out, in an oblique way, the existential echoes of their elders. The figure itself was seen only as an isolated, forlorn object in a hostile environment. The power of de Kooning's image was, in these painters, generally dissipated by literalism, sentimentalism abetted by the loose expressionist technique they had adopted. The incongruities of the approach are still not apparent to most painters trying to reconcile the obviously irreconcilable techniques of figure painting and abstract expressionism.

The other mode — the confections of artists harking back to the mordant jokes of the Dadaists — incorporated de Kooning's satiric overtones (for instance, the cut-out of a lipsticked, toothy mouth in de Kooning's "Woman" has turned up in many a young neo-Dada collage) as well as his slapdash painting technique. The assimilation of widely varying materials within an image typical of de Kooning was used by these younger artists to good purpose.

I mention these two tendencies in passing only to illustrate de Kooning's scope and his ability to focus problems inherent in the Western modern tradition for other painters. De Kooning as a catalytic agent remains important.

9 : Dim Oriental Echoes

THE ECHO of Zen Buddhism in contemporary painting is exceedingly dim and requires careful tracking. Essentially, both European and American postwar painting evolves within the Western tradition. But as in past epochs, from the Middle Ages on, Orientalism has consistently attracted artists. There have been moments when the influence of the East — no matter how mistakenly applied by writers and painters — has assumed significant proportions in Western art.

Barr justifiably linked Existentialism and Zen as two tendencies of thought that took on special allure immediately after the war. Obviously Zen, with its ambiguous intricacies, could not be grasped as readily by Western minds as Existentialism. But total comprehension was not necessary. It was enough that the strangeness of Zen, its radically different approach to reality, infiltrated the minds of artists. Artists have been aware of Zen because they sensed a need for elements missing in the inherited Western tradition. On the whole they made no attempt to study Zen closely, or even to ponder its philosophical implications. They took the stimulus they needed from Zen's exotic character — just enough to set their imaginations racing, not enough to ensnare them in the profound difficulties Zen presents to the Western mind.

The postwar mood that nurtured the pessimistic thoughts of Existentialists brought many young minds to consider Eastern philosophies. In their eyes, both Existentialism and Zen represented a revolt from the overintellectualized, metaphysical philosophies dominating Western culture. A description by Louis Pauwels sums up the mood of large numbers of young intellectuals in both Europe and the United States during and after the war:

I was twenty years old in 1940, in the debacle. I belonged to a generation that had seen a world wreck itself; that was cut off from the past and doubted the future. . . . During the war I took refuge in Hinduism . . . It was my wilderness. I lived there in absolute resistance. Let's not look for the point of departure in history and among men: it always escapes. Let's look for it in ourselves. Let's be of this world as if we weren't of this world. Nothing seemed more beautiful than the plunging bird in the Bhagavad-Gita "who plunged and remounted without wetting his plumage." Of the events against which we could do nothing, I told myself, let's see to it that they can do nothing against us. I installed myself on the ceiling, seated in lotus on a cloud come from the Orient . . . Later, just after

the Liberation, I took a master. I became a disciple of Gurdjieff.
I worked to separate myself from my emotions, my sentiments, my enthusiasms in order to find in the beyond something immobile and permanent; a mute, anonymous, transcendent presence that would console me for the absurdity of the world. . . . I pushed to their extreme consequences this sentiment of exile, this need of radical revolt expressed in literary reviews around 1947 when they spoke of "metaphysical inquietude," which was the difficult heritage of my generation.[1]

Superficially, the discussions in literary reviews and among artists linked Zen and Existentialism because both were apparently in search of *concrete* experience divested of the elaborate rhetoric of metaphysical philosophies. Individual responsibility, stress on intuition, and opposition to analytical or logical techniques of thought seemed common to both philosophies to the disillusioned generation. Self-recognition through concrete experience: an ideal tangible enough to inflame imaginations.

Very little was known of Zen, especially in America, where it enjoyed even a greater vogue than in Europe. But an artist needed only to see a few phrases by Dr. Suzuki to be stimulated. "Zen demands of the disciple that he see his own physiognomy, his original physiognomy" — such a phrase was sufficient. Subtleties such as the difference between the "self" of the Eastern thinker and the "self" of the West were left to savants. It was enough to know that a search for self was basic to both philosophies.

The modern Western *rapprochement* with Oriental aesthetics has a long history (the encyclopedists of the eighteenth century, for instance, were fascinated with Orientalia). In relation to the contemporary attitude, however, the immediate source is in the nineteenth century. Baudelaire's espousal of analogy and psychological correspondences came close to an Eastern point of view in that it defied a materialist tradition and moved toward a fusion of the artist with nature, or the cosmos. "The whole visible universe is only a store of images and signs to which the imagination accords a relative place and value."

The sage Oriental artist knows better than to pit himself against nature. Even Baudelaire's position keeps him *outside* of nature, looking for the way in. Yet, his idea of analogy is similar to the Oriental. In the formal tradition of Japanese painting, teaching was done by means of analogy. "Storks' legs are as pine branches; Fujiyama as the forehead of a beautiful woman, an elephant's eye as an orchid plant." Baudelaire and his symbolist followers, in spurning established relations between the material world and the artist, helped provide the foundation of abstract painting.

After the end of the nineteenth century and long before Zen became a voguish preoccupation, painters and writers already groped instinctively toward the ideas later associated with the East. Whether accurately or not, the writer who "discovers" Heraclitus in *Camera Work* in 1910 senses the drift toward Eastern aesthetics. To many uninformed readers Heraclitus's paradoxes seem close in spirit to Zen Buddhist riddles. (It is not important to my discussion whether Heraclitus has been taken out of context and misread. I am only trying to show the kind of thought processes at work — not the accuracy of the data used.) "All

things come out of the one and the one out of all things,"
Heraclitus is supposed to have said. "The way up and the
way down is one and the same thing." He was also said to
have characterized his whole philosophy in two Greek
words translated "I have sought for myself." These and
other raisins picked out of Heraclitus's philosophy served
to confirm the drift of Western art theory toward the
Orient.

What was mistily, instinctively apprehended by Western
painters were the Zen ideas of the void, of vast spaces in
which man is but a feather, of silences, of "no-mind," or
the banishment of fixed patterns of thought. As Mark Tobey, one of the few painters intimately acquainted with
Zen, remarked, his experience in the Orient taught him that
a deep absorption in nature enabled him to "get out of the
way." In other words, sustained by concentration, his self
becomes permeated with essences in nature and "nature
takes over." In Tobey and several others, this was not entirely a subjective technique, but rather a flight toward
the higher goal — arrived at by discipline — in which the
identity of the artist becomes mingled with the vitality of
that which he is expressing.

Interest in Zen on the part of visual artists and writers
was as much directed to style as to content. The abbreviated, fragmented forms of Zen writings and the immediacy of brush painting influenced by Zen attracted them. In
the case of writings, both Chinese Tao and Zen Buddhism
speak in the poetic, nonlogical idiom an artist instinctively
understands. A swift poetic parable can say more to an artist than a philosophical tract, which is why, for instance,

Kafka is far more important to contemporary artists than any discursive philosopher could be. The contemporary abstract painter would recognize the following two examples of Oriental writing as related to his own conceptions. Both fragments are in Arthur Waley's book *Three Ways of Thought in Ancient China* and are in the chapter on Chuang Tzu called "The Realm of Nothing Whatever." [2]

The first is about a king who had a carver named Ting who was carving a bull for him. "Wonderful," said the king, "I could never have believed that the art of carving could reach such a point as this."

"I am a lover of Tao," replied Ting, putting away his knife, "and have succeeded in applying it to the art of carving. When I first began to carve I fixed my gaze on the animal before me. After three years I no longer saw it as a whole bull, but as a thing already divided into parts. Nowadays I no longer see it with the eye; I merely apprehend it with the soul. My sense-organs are in abeyance, but my soul still works."

In the second, Waley quotes the following Taoist statement: "The eye is a menace to clear sight, the ear is a menace to subtle hearing, the mind is a menace to wisdom, every organ of the senses is a menace to its own capacity. Sad is it indeed that man should look upon these seats of menace as his greatest treasure."

Man's greatest treasure, according to Chang Tzu, is his Inward Vision, described by Waley as "a generalized perception that can come into play only when the distinction between 'inside' and 'outside,' between 'self' and 'things,' between 'this' and 'that,' has been entirely obliterated."

Something of that "Inward Vision" appeared in the paintings of Tobey and Pollock, who both generalized, tried to get "inside" their paintings. Pollock wrote in 1947: "On the floor I am more at ease, I feel nearer, more a part of the painting since this way I can walk around it, work from four sides and literally be *in* the painting." [3] Tobey, in his "white writing," also painted himself into his paintings. He had realized in the thirties, after his trip to China and Japan, that "depth is something felt rather than seen" and that "space is everywhere and anywhere." In his white-writing painting, where there was no closed system of perspective, no solid forms — only light and rhythm — he was expressing his self within the perpetual movement and greater harmony he felt in the cosmos.

The flux of all within space was declared by many of the painters who had finally rejected classical perspective. A process of rejection had begun with Goya. Throughout the nineteenth century, painters consciously questioned the canons of Renaissance perspective, sought alternative attitudes toward picture space. But it remained for the painters of the twentieth century to make a final break. For them there was no longer a fixed point of focus. Space was conceived by Kline, de Kooning, Guston, Still, Rothko and others as an interminable extension, an element that was at once inside and outside the painting. It could no longer be expressed in the Renaissance perspective cube with its vanishing points, but had to be expressed in its ultimate ambiguity.

In another way, the Oriental aspect of American painting has inspired considerable commentary linking the work of "calligraphic" American painters with that of Japanese calligraphists. The natural association is made, of course, with the work of Franz Kline, but Tobey, Pollock, Guston, Gottlieb, Brooks and even de Kooning have been discussed as vaguely related to contemporary Japanese painting, particularly the new school of "abstract calligraphy." The Japanese themselves bow deeply to the work of Franz Kline, recognizing kinship.

In a sense the development of cursive and linear modes was a natural development, from Gauguin to Matisse, to the automatistic surrealists (Masson and Ernst above all), to the current linear abstract painters. The emphasis on "handwriting" coincided with the emphasis on the individual. Nothing can be more autographic than an autograph.

Our so-called calligraphic painters share only one trait with the Japanese calligraphists: a solipsistic feeling toward the universe. The ways in which they differ are worth examining.

Originally, Japanese characters were based on the Chinese, which were ideographic, or symbols. (The form was their meaning.) Later, a phonetic alphabet of forty-seven characters, or signs, was developed. The modern Japanese "abstract calligraphers" use both. When they begin with a classical symbol, they are merely heightening an already existent symbol. When they begin with a phonetic character, they base their compositions on the literal meaning of the word. Ultimately, then, their paintings are more or less dependent on given symbolizations, and are not purely formal.

Unlike us, the Japanese inherited a tradition that benev-

olently provided for abstract, symbolic exigencies. Without going into the profound philosophies nurturing Oriental art, it is still possible to view the present abstract
calligraphy in the light of centuries of painting governed
by canon. There were some seventy-two laws governing
Japanese classical painting. They range from explicit in-
structions in brushwork to a lexicon of prototypal forms.
There were also broader governing principles, such as the
principle of Sei Do, or Living Movement. As a psychological principle, it is akin to the Western concept of *Einfüh-
lung,* or empathy. The artist is expected to find correspondences between himself and the object contemplated, even
an inanimate object, by "feeling into" the pure nature of
his subject.

How such a principle is creatively applied by the classical Japanese artist can be seen in Henry P. Bowie's *On the
Laws of Japanese Painting:* [4]

The artist Buncho being requested to paint a crow flying
across four sliding door panels, after much reflection, painted
the bird in the act of disappearing from the last of these subdivisions, the space of the other three suggesting rapid flight
which the crow had already accomplished, and the law of pro-
portion (Ichi), or orderly arrangement, thus observed was uni-
versally applauded.

A tradition of symbolism, or abstraction, then, was
ready-made for the contemporary Japanese artist, while
for us, it had to be created. Perspective and imitative realism were the enemies the twentieth-century painter had to
rout, and he was hampered by a deplorably analytic cul-

ture. The Western artist tends to approach art as if it were an organism for dissection, for analysis, for presenting "meaning," while for the Japanese artist, a symbol is not set off between mental parentheses of analysis. For him a symbol is organic, not requiring verbal autopsies.

The contemporary American abstract painter is still struggling with Western traditions, no matter how much he tries to evade them. What is recognized as "handwriting" in many contemporary paintings or what appear to be "ideograms" (as Kline's paintings have sometimes been called) represent more the process of *search* for symbol than symbol itself.

IO : Calligraphic Illusions

IN SOME ARTISTS the process of search for symbol is slow, meditative. Even if at a certain moment the canvas began to appear to one American after another as an arena in which to act, for others it was more like a Greek stage on which action was carried out slowly, ceremoniously.

For Franz Kline, the process was a swift, instinctual force. Very little intervened between his inspiration and his act. One painting was not a means toward another. On the contrary, each of the stark signs he painted, each insurgent gesture, was like a letter in a private alphabet, standing singly and inviolably.

When, toward 1950, the large black and white paintings first appeared, there was much speculation as to what they were about. Some saw trestles, bridges and great engineering feats reflected in Kline's black tracery.

Others saw an extension of Oriental calligraphy. Still others felt that Kline evoked analogy to the brutal aspects of contemporary life; the violent blacks were cicatrices.

Oriental analogies are farfetched. Kline does not paint giant characters. His themes are never established in the defined terms an Eastern symbolic art requires. As for the "calligraphic" qualities, physically speaking, that is pure illusion. Kline's streamers of line are not achieved in a single gesture. They are built up (they would have to be, in the huge scale he usually elects) and refined before they take their place in relation to white interstices. Even such a swift painting as "Vawdavitch, 1955" has its "worked" blacks.

As for seeing the Third Avenue "el" and Brooklyn Bridge in his paintings, I think not. Allusion is minimal in Kline's paintings. Kline's basic drive is to call up forms that are inherently dynamic or shocking. These huge blacknesses are to work psychologically on the viewer.

Like Pollock, Kline is an insistent *tabula rasa* painter. As far as I know, he went through none of the transitional involvement with primitive art and myth, but plunged directly into abstraction. Sacrificing shadings and details, Kline's astringent abstract style was geared from the first to stun, to shock slumbering senses into cognizance of a particular experience: that of the suddenly perceived sign in the wilderness.

The black signals Kline shoots across the raw white of canvas span a wilderness. They hurtle through an emptiness that can be likened to a desert. They veer off into a space more massive than the human eye can perceive and

FRANZ KLINE, *Vawdavitch*, 1955. Oil, 62 x 80½.

(Fairweather-Hardin Gallery, Chicago)

are unbounded by conventional space determinants such as horizon lines and orderly verticals. To this extent only does Kline have something in common with Buncho.

The vertiginous rush of Kline's signs represent "forces" which are unnamed, just as the imaginary roar and the stillness of the desert cannot be named. Kline's desert is urban, of course, but no less overwhelming.

What gives Kline's image its forceful character is its scale. Why are the Easter Island monolithic heads more ominous than a Roman god standing on a piazza? Is it not because the stone heads, seeming to force their way up from the rocky plain like giant plants, are so many times greater than human measure that they override even the horizon? These forms stir apprehension: it is superhuman to subdue a horizon. Kline's paintings in their large scale achieve a similar effect. The arms of a Kline form, like giant blades, cut into a space foreign to the human sense of scale.

In 1958, Kline broadened his approach, including both color and tone. By tone, Kline means the intermediary between the blackest of black, and white. In certain of the 1958 paintings, such as "Siegfried," Kline seemed to have reached the limit of the superhuman sign. The large panels of billowing black seek Wagnerian crescendo. They crawl in stormy masses from a pitlike ground to sky, and in a way are reminiscent of Tintoretto's plague scenes in their spiraling masses. Unwilling to part with the throttling drama of his black-and-white signs paintings, Kline in these predominantly black and dark-

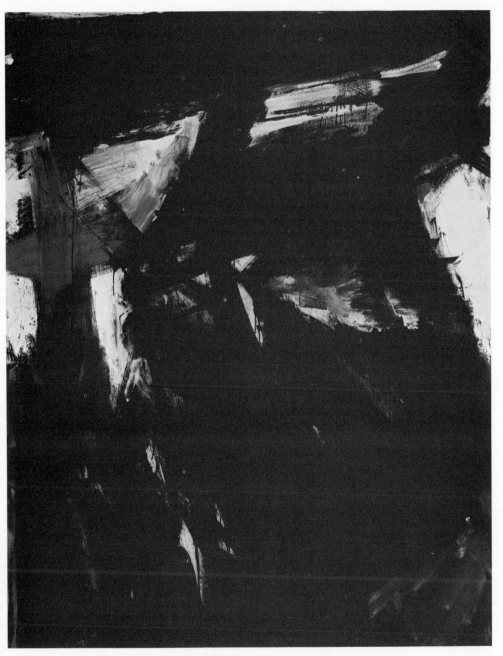

FRANZ KLINE, *Siegfried,* 1958. Oil, 103 x 81.

(*Carnegie Institute, Pittsburgh*)

gray canvases attempted to give reality to a holocaust of speeding winds and dark clouds.

Still, Kline's reality is spelled out in the alphabet of shooting forms he has evolved, and each one registers sharply. They are symbols of tensions, taut and excited, but tensions between what polar entities? His art is too immediate, too instinctual for us to be able to name them.

Mark Tobey, on the other hand, is a meditative painter, an intimist. As his work has unfolded since the early 1930's, a definite dialectic has become clear. He is painting a continuum. More than any other American painter, he has grasped and assimilated Oriental aesthetics, and his influence, while indirect, is admitted by several of the outstanding younger painters.

Tobey was already in his forties when he went to the Orient. It was a natural step for him. His earliest reflections led him to a vision of life as ever-renewing and the cosmos as a "greater unity." Like the pre-Socratic Greeks, Tobey thought of a world in eternal motion, refusing to accept the modern Western concept of life as "a series of terminations." In the East, where Tao suggests the vital force of constant regeneration, Tobey found confirmation.

There, Tobey learned of his innate affinity for dynamic line rather than mass. He belongs by temperament to the special family constant in art history that has known the obsessive, animating power of line. That family includes Leonardo (his turbulent late drawings of deluges), the Celtic illustrators, Kandinsky and Klee, as well as the Chinese and Japanese calligraphers.

In Tobey's new conception of painting evolved in the 1930's, the subject was to be the interrelation of macrocosm and microcosm. His moment of dialectic insight was recorded in a published letter:

"While in Japan sitting on the floor of a room looking over an intimate garden with flowers blooming and dragonflies hovering in space, I sensed that this small world almost underfoot had a validity all its own, but must be realized and appreciated from its own level in space." [1]

In charting his complex course between the smaller and greater worlds, Tobey drew on his inherent respect for the intimate; for that which in its reduction, compression, and minute detail gains in intensity. He understood early what many painters have come to understand since: that imaginative man can shift his perspective endlessly. He can see a surface closely, in all its dense detail, or he can see it from a distance in its integrity.

Painters before him, and poets, had known of this psychological slipping from one range of vision to another. They indicated vastness by enumerating miscroscopic detail, or by eliminating all detail. Both perspectives, both ways of interpreting the universe, are finally equal. Tobey had known how to use this flexible dialectic so that in a single picture, eye and mind can shift from climate to climate, region to region, space to space — what he calls "multiple margins of space" — while remaining within the intimate precincts of Tobey's hermetic universe.

Having discovered in the Orient that he could "write" his feelings, Tobey made line the carrier of his notion of continuum. By brushing layer upon layer of delicate line

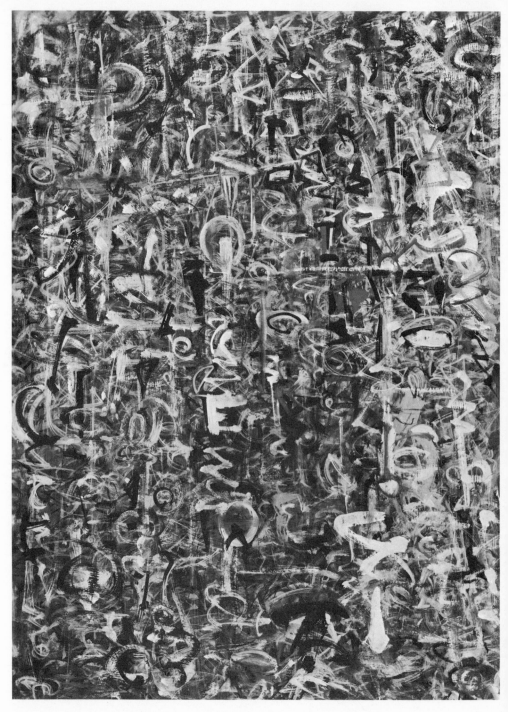

MARK TOBEY, *Tundra*, 1944. Tempera, 24 x 16½.

(*Collection of Mr. and Mrs. Roy Neuberger*)

in flowing rhythms in the famous white-writing paintings, he could symbolize his Heraclitan conviction that all
things come out of the one, the one out of all things. His
medium — tempera — could easily suggest fluidity.

Although the classical meander that has laced itself
through all art epochs is Tobey's principal means, he
often uses it to create mass, only it is microscopic mass he
attains. Sometimes his paintings are composed of floating
planes, fragments that drift inexorably into characteristic
patterns. Each of his paintings has a point of focus, and as
"all-over" as they may seem, there is always an internal
logic to the progressions of forms and skeins of line.

In "writing" his paintings Tobey introduced a cursive
mode now very popular. It was not only his training in calligraphy that brought him to this art of time-space. It was
his deep engagement with music as well. His effort to set
up specific rhythms in his paintings depends as much on his
musical as his visual sensibility.

The specific musical character of certain of Tobey's
paintings is given in an equivalent to *sostenuto*. If a musician holds a note for an instant longer than our expecta-
tion, he changes our experience. We are moved by a different force, one which holds time suspended and makes it
"concrete." Tobey arrives at his *sostenuto* — the note carried to its fullest value — by taking small elements and
building them in steadily advancing rhythms until they
establish a continuum saturated with time.

Although there are melodic outbursts in Tobey's linear
paintings, finally, the whole appears evenly massed. Tobey has indicated that his paintings must be regarded again

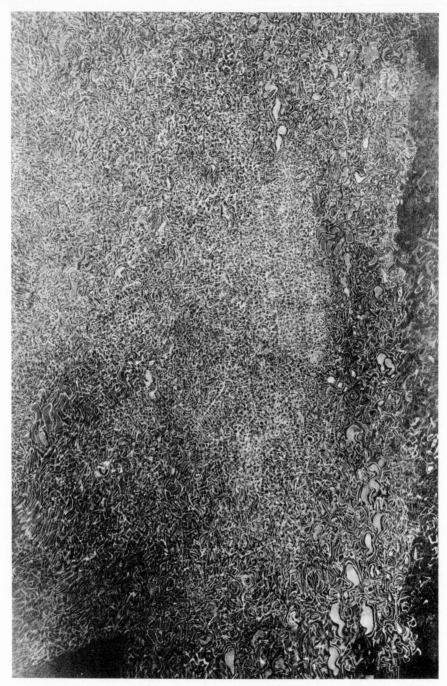

MARK TOBEY, *Canticle*, 1954. Casein, 17¼ x 11½.

(*Collection of the Sara Roby Foundation, New York*)

and again since no single contrasting image should remain
with the beholder.

In this, he is faithful to the mysteriously static art of the East. It is an absolute peculiarly Eastern, and not widely appreciated in America. The painter Ad Reinhardt, who in his own way is steeped in Oriental philosophy and regularly provides the dissenting voice in the "informal" chorus, described this Eastern aesthetic — and his own convictions — in an article called "Timeless in Asia" in *Art News,* January 1960:

If there is one thing to say about Asia's art then, it is about its timelessness, its monotony, its inaction, its quietness, its dignity, its negativity . . . Nowhere in world art has it been clearer than in Asia that anything irrational, momentary, spontaneous, unconscious, primitive, expressionist, accidental or informal, cannot be called serious art. Only blankness, complete awareness, disinterestedness; the "artist as artist" only, of one and rational mind, "vacant and spiritual, empty and marvelous," in symmetries and regularities only; the changeless "human content," the timeless "supreme principle," the ageless "universal formula" of art, nothing else.

Recognizing the "one schemata behind all schematas" in the changeless art of Asia, Reinhardt has sought a timeless distance in his own paintings. His luminous dark purple, purple-black and silver-black canvases have to be sensed rather than seen. So reticent are the schematic crossbars and verticals in these paintings that they become "presences" rather than painted surfaces. The extremely moving darkness in Reinhardt's recent paintings fulfills his longing for an absolute, for the one schemata behind all schematas.

The "distance" or meditative foundation in the work of Tobey was never achieved by the other outstanding linearist, Pollock. Pollock was a man of turbulent impulse whose search for the symbols of existence, for a whole, was hampered by many beginnings, many failures.

His paintings reveal a man of enormous appetite, forced to check the successions of sensation which came upon him with greater rapidity than he could accommodate. He was forced to move now in one direction, now another to even out the ragged pace of his maturing.

After Pollock's mythical and surreal images ceased to satisfy him, he was extremely restless. But he had made two important discoveries: He found he could detach line from forms, creating another dimension. And he found that if he bore out his frenzy in abstract terms, covering the surface at all costs, he could find an intensity equivalent to his emotion.

Pollock's discovery of line was crucial. Leaving behind the objects which had filled and made heavy the lines in his mythical paintings, Pollock was able to fulfill a pressing temperamental need. He was able to give rein to his large fund of lyrical response and create the deeply desired unity.

His early nonobjective paintings, such as "Shimmering Substance" (1946), were composed of hundreds of fat, curling strokes, intertwining equally over the surface, their yellowish masses underridden with somewhat darker strokes. Pollock's tendency to closure is seen in the way the

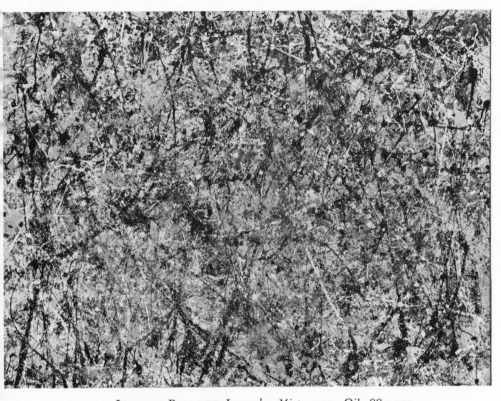

JACKSON POLLOCK, *Lavender Mist,* 1950. Oil, 88 x 119.

(*Collection of Alfonso Ossorio, East Hampton, New York*)

circular lines move inward, always closing off the edges. The barbaric interlace which recurs throughout history finds its modern exponent in Pollock. But unlike Tobey's quiet, continuing absorption, Pollock's spirit was like a wild fly, transcribing huge arcs on a rain-veiled window, answering a compelling instinctive circular urge.

Pollock's affinity for the arabesque, that ornamental figure which always returns to its source no matter how intricate its trajectory, is obvious in the group of paintings done between 1947 and 1952 which are so overwhelmingly, obsessively intricate. In them, the flow of spirit, the rustling, murmuring, sighing intensity, the sealike rhythms which are sustained from one canvas to the next come closest to an integral, unified vision. It is apparent that within the variations Pollock tried, there was always a form-will that insisted on the return of the line, no matter how freely drawn, how densely woven, or how many vagaries that line was permitted.

But along with this sense of the powerful and ingenious personality behind these works, one feels the obsessive and perhaps desperate repetition — a repetition not nourished by a philosophic concept of flux, as in the case of Tobey, but the by-product of a search for something further. The great climatic paintings which Clement Greenberg says were complete fulfillment for Pollock were possibly merely a pause. His restlessness and dissatisfaction with the "drip" paintings appear in his final works. In them, Pollock dallied again with the figure and symbol, or sought to recapitulate all his previous discoveries in a single canvas. He was hesitant and searching, wandering in his past and

JACKSON POLLOCK, *Number 14*, 1951. Oil, 57½ x 106.

(*Collection of Lee Krasner Pollock, Springs, East Hampton, New York*)

seeking the clue to himself. The essential difference between his work and Tobey's is precisely that Pollock was one of the painters to whom the canvas became, for a time, "an arena in which to act." But the action in itself probably did not satisfy him.

Pollock's linearism differs from Tobey's not only in scale but in structure. The additions of hundreds of layers of line in Pollock's "symphonic" works serve to structure space in a dense but readable series of planes. To the extent that he created these masses, which can be read from the picture plane to the ground plane in sequence, Pollock remained in the Western tradition. His lines have none of the finality of the Oriental line. His was an empirical approach, unprepared by any a priori philosophy.

II : European Counterpoint

II : The Postwar Avant-Garde
: in Europe

I N 1924 Paul Klee wrote: "What artist does not yearn to dwell near the mind, or heart of creation itself, that prime mover of events in time and space." He dreamed of "a work of quite exceptional breadth, covering the entire realm of subject, content and style," adding, "It's a good idea from time to time to imagine the possibility of such an achievement vague as it may seem today." [1]

The possibility was imagined in postwar Europe, as it was in the United States. To artists everywhere it was no longer a vague achievement to be longed for but a realizable ideal in painting. The mind and heart of creation itself seemed accessible.

The intense self-absorption of painters and critics in America after the war tended to obscure affinities between European and American tendencies. Still today, both sides indulge in futile polemics about who got there first. American art magazines frequently wrote themselves congratulatory and nationalistic panegyrics, celebrating what they liked to call the "breakthrough." Europe was undergoing a similar experience. The impetuous expressionism, termed abstract in the United States, appeared in Europe under the large heading of "informalism." Naturally, there were differences. There was a certain delay — due to political circumstance in Europe — in European momentum. But the same spirit of revolt and rejection of the past could be found simultaneously in New York and Paris.

The problem of "influences" (American on European painting particularly) can be jettisoned conveniently, if we bear in mind that there was a young generation in Europe eager to assimilate whatever seemed radically different from the past. First there was a will to discover new territory. Then came the "influence." It is the attitude, the will, that must be considered.

As France remained the strongest center, postwar European art can be seen in its light. Traditionally the French painter has been assigned the role of the rationalist in paint. Many art historians and critics have ignored recurrent expressionist tendencies in the history of French painting in order to sustain a dubious thesis of French painterly logic.

The postwar French painter — particularly the young painter — was thoroughly bored with the designation. He identified logical constructions, cuisine and the defined spaces inherited from the cubists and nonobjective painters with a _cul de sac_ past. Striking out for the freedom of ambiguity, the new French painter attacked his canvas as an adversary, just as the American abstract expressionist did, sweeping over it with a variety of media; uninhibited "calligraphic" brushstrokes instead of solidly defined forms; signs rather than symbols, and surfaces rather than built-up perspective structures. This new painting that rejected cubism, neoplasticism, and even the expressionism of Soutine came to be called among other things *tachisme,* deriving from the French word meaning stain or spot. Like most brand names for new painting imagery, the word was first used derisively.

The Parisian art world was profoundly shocked. Jean Cassou, director of the Museum of Modern Art in Paris, deplored the faintness of the *esprit latin,* and in a public lecture as late as 1954, was still complaining that French painting was being overrun by what he called the "northern personality." M. Cassou apparently forgot that the extravagances of French baroque and rococo grew just as certainly from the *esprit latin* as did the contained logic of cubism. The so-called northern personality, by which M. Cassou evidently meant expressionist, was indeed overrunning Europe and America, but in quite a different manner than M. Cassou could then imagine.

The extent of changing attitudes to painting, at least among the French avant-garde, was indicated by an abrupt turning in critical writing — a turning away from sober art historical and formal methods toward writing that was meant to be equivalent to the "informal" spirit. One critic, protesting traditional French cuisine, issued a proclamation of "imaginary art" where "the motor element, principal agent of propulsion into the unrevealed," would be prime, and where the traditional concerns of *esprit latin* patriots would be deliberately flouted. Suddenly, the word *liberté* slipped away from its conventional meaning and became a sign for an ideal and scarcely defined freedom beyond the bounds of reason. Immediacy, spontaneity, instantaneity became key words of praise.

As in the United States, the Oriental influence was cited in relation to the linear quality of many of the tachiste paintings with their whirling, crisscrossing, hurtling lines, or their large single marks resembling characters. Occasionally, at least after 1950, a French critic would throw a hasty glance at America, but the French avant-garde, like the American, had ambivalent feelings, sometimes claiming kinship, sometimes disclaiming any common ground.

The critics who lent their support to the "new" painting in Paris were, for the most part, men who had seen at least a dozen movements come and go. They had been through the weary years in which abstraction as conceived by the cubists seemed to freeze into academicism. They saw surrealism fall into a Technicolor dreamworld, never to emerge. And they saw Mondrian's style turned into "concrete" art, brutalized by countless imitators. What else was there but to hope for a cathartic movement which could at the very least convey vivid emotion? Back to the Celts, the Africans, the Easter Islanders — anywhere that direct emotion was unsullied by cerebralism.

The extreme of the *tabula rasa* psychology was expressed by Michel Tapié, critic and dealer, who wrote copiously about what he called *l'art autre* (other art), a term that has gained currency in Europe and still covers a multitude of begged questions.[2] Tapié was quick to grasp the mood of artists not only of his native Paris and the rest of Europe, but in New York, San Francisco and Japan as well. It was through his initiative that the work of Jackson Pollock was first shown in Paris in 1953.

Tapié's platform called for a conscious denial of classicism and a leap into the exalted state of imagination desired by all romantics. The salient words in his statements — and those of artists in his group — are the familiar infinity-longing words such as *l'inconnu, le transcendement* and *l'insaisissable* — the unknown, the transcendent and the ungraspable. He tended to use these phrases in an incantatory high-priest tone where the structure of language was treated with cavalier indifference, much as the structure of form and color in painting was willfully ignored or abused by overenthusiastic converts.

An admirer of Dada, Tapié has never abandoned the chain of renunciations it advocated. In his view, idolatry of the past must be totally forsaken in order for "other" art to exist. Ironically, Dada itself has a substantial past and much of the recent reprise of Dada mannerisms smacks of the same academicism the tachistes claimed the more conventional abstract painters represented. An interesting sidelight is that there has been a consistent interaction between Europe and America since the days when Picabia and Duchamp were in New York together. The recent European Dadaist activity probably preceded its reflux in the United States which seemed to reach its climax in 1961.

The diction of critics such as Tapié appealed to the young impatient painters he addressed. He spoke of a kind of painting in which "the individual is left with the possibility of his Paroxysm." The agony of paroxysms, he suggested, will bring forth a measure of truth from "primordial matter." This orgiastic element already existed in the work of several painters Tapié championed. It remained for him to exaggerate "primordial urges" and to contrive an elaborate superstructure of theory in which he freely transposed terms from topology, physics and philosophy, resorting to obscurantism when the principles he was discussing were larger than his technical knowledge could accommodate.

Many Parisian critics were recasting parent ideas from Dada and surrealism into lapidary prose-poems. Large sections of surrealist theory were lifted whole from the past and dropped amidst the toiling postwar avant-garde. So much so that André Breton came, like Mephistopheles, to claim his own, sponsoring several exhibitions of tachiste paintings by young artists. Breton, in waging his war against the conventional *esprit latin* and in trying to identify French painting with its Celtic rather than its Greco-Roman past, reached out as far as the Orient. The "great exploit" of modern art, he wrote in 1954, is to fight the world of appearance, to reject all that is "cortical" in order to find the marrow, the essence, the guts of things as Eastern artists had done. Discussing one painter, he wrote, "Without wishing it, this art renews the lesson of the Extreme Orient, that of the works of Zen."[3] And, he added with mock modesty: "I think that there is nothing there to deny my own presumptions at the time of the origin of Surrealism, in direct rapport with automatic writing, that *that* is the ineluctable future of painting." Breton defers only to Kandinsky, acknowledging Kandinsky's principle of "inner necessity" as the source of art.

The orgiastic, the intuitional, the cosmic, the transcendent — call it what you will — the principle determining postwar Western painting was emphatically rebellious and anticlassical. The need for rebellion appeared long before resulting works of art. The avant-garde necessity occurred to painters in every country in Europe. Paris was still the navel of the European art world in 1946 and young painters from Italy, Holland, Belgium, Spain, Scandinavia and Great Britain made haste to come into contact with the greater world of art.

Whether they arrived in 1946, in time to witness the outrage of critics and public before Dubuffet's explosive exhibition; or in 1948, in time to hear raging arguments between the semiabstract painters and their partisans, and the new minority rebels; or in 1950, in time to hear the loud exhortations of critics like Tapié, and to hear about Jackson Pollock and the Japanese calligraphers, and the quarrels between partisans of "cold" abstraction with those of "warm" abstraction, the young painters who came to Paris were ripe for conversion.

To better understand the whirlwind diffusion of informal painting, it is instructive to look briefly at the postwar history of other countries in Europe besides France — Italy, for instance. Fascist Italy was isolated from the European mainstream. Only one advanced group managed to survive before the war: the geometric abstractionists in Milan led by painters such as Soldati and Magnelli. Other painters in Florence or Rome struggled to keep in touch with Paris, and some of the older generation managed to hold on to the lessons of cubism despite the reactionary prewar climate. But the young generation — those who in 1945 were less than twenty years old, or who were nearing thirty but had been delayed in their painting by the war — knew next to nothing of what had happened in Paris. In 1946, when Professor Lionello Venturi returned to Italy, he staged an exhibition of color reproductions of the Impressionists in the modern museum in Rome, and for countless younger painters, it was their first exposure to "modern" art.

Intelligent younger men eagerly tracked down magazines and books telling of the twentieth-century movements in painting, and much of their development depended on how much literature they could find. The actual works of art by Miró or Picasso or Mondrian were unknown.

They were, of course, familiar with their own avant-garde tradition embodied in the Futurist movement. Many of the developments in the postwar avant-garde in Italy were implicit in Futurist theories. For instance, Marinetti had already pointed the way to informalism when he said in his *Technical Manifesto of Futurist Literature* in 1910: "Analogy is nothing more than the immense love that reunites distant things, apparently different and hostile. By means of vast analogies this orchestral style, at the same time polychrome, polyphonic and polymorphic, can embrace the life of matter."

The Futurist emphasis on experiment, and above all on the incorporation of unaccustomed materials (to combat academic elegance), was to affect postwar Italian painting through the work of Alberto Burri. Almost certainly Burri was urged beyond the limits of oil painting by his memory of Futurist tenets, and by his acquaintance with one of the younger Futurists, Enrico Prampolini.

Prampolini, who had come late to the movement, had sustained his interest between the wars. His incorporation of surrealism, seen in constructions made with non-art materials, led him, after the war, to experiments that were considered very daring by the Romans in the late 1940's.

After beginning to paint in the United States as a prisoner of war, Burri returned to Rome and became associated with the group led by Prampolini called Origine. Toward 1949, his abstractions became very heavy, painted thickly, scored and sculptured, and built up with sand and other extraneous materials.

These experiments with heavy materials led him toward 1950 into the renunciation of oil paint. Instead of brushes and paint, Burri began to compose with burlap sacking which he stitched together, arranged in somber sequences on tarry grounds. By means of this revolutionary collage technique, Burri attracted attention. Scores of younger men — those who were too young to have participated in the war — began to see a way to express their will be rebel in the use of unorthodox materials. Burri had the same influence on his younger contemporaries that Antonio Tapiès was to have five years later on his Spanish contemporaries who, in Franco Spain, were cut off from the mainstream of European art history for even longer than the Italians had been.

The immediate postwar reaction in Rome belongs to the European history of total disenchantment with prewar institutions. A deep-rooted sense of stagnation, of cultural isolation irritated one young group of artists who in 1947 wrote an impassioned manifesto pleading for a "European language of pure form." Piero Dorazio has written that "this manifesto of formalism was the first stand of the young artists in defense of the spirit and international tradition of modern art against the nationalist and realist tradition resumed immediately after the war." [4]

Kandinsky, Mondrian, Picasso and Klee: the first stage in re-education for the young. Then surrealism. Then mild distortions of cubism. For some, around 1952, neo-realism. And finally, between 1950 and 1953, abstract expressionism, or informalism. Dorazio's remarks, though referring only to the Italians, and only to painting, could be extended for other countries and other arts. Internationalism became an urgent necessity, stressed increasingly in the arts as nationalism threatened once again in politics. This desperate need for universality is more serious and significant than many cynical observers concede. Too often it is thought to be a useful international-commercial *rapprochement;* or the result merely of increasing mass-media communication. A young Spanish or Italian or Polish painter, however, often arrives at his internationalism through moral and philosophical necessity.

All the sources of twentieth-century art were discovered and used by restless young painters. Even where divergent developments occurred, the ultimate result was international. The "northern personality" asserted itself in the Cobra group, for instance, but the group was eventually dissolved and several of its members are now identified with the School of Paris.

Cobra — an abbreviation of Copenhagen, Brussels and Amsterdam, the three centers from which its members came — was organized in the late 1940's.[5] Its members were interested in expressionist fantasy, in surrealism, in Klee, Miró and expressionist phases of Picasso. Their paintings appeared to be within the northern expressionist tradition, nurtured by dark tales of trolls and monsters as well as Munch and Van Gogh. In reality, it was equally close in spirit to a sister movement in Paris. At the same time Asger Jorn or Karel Appel were depicting childlike monsters and hybrid animals, Paris was being scandalized by *l'art brut* — the work of children and madmen raised by Dubuffet as a barricade against stagnant abstract art.

Much has been made of the Cobra movement as an independent postwar phenomenon. My own impression is that the young men who banded together had already been initiated into prewar expressionism in the course of their studies and that their first distorted images of children and animals came directly from German expressionism.

Their variations, tinged with surrealism, occurred only

after considerable interchange among themselves and their French contemporaries. We are told that the idea of founding the Cobra group occurred to several of its members as they sat around a café table in Paris in 1948. This would mean that they were familiar with Dubuffet's *succès de scandale*. His eccentricities probably inspired them to accentuate their own.

The significance of the Cobra painters lies mainly in their insistence on figurative symbolism. They provided in northern Europe the dissenting voice to academic abstraction that Francis Bacon furnished in England. As horror-ridden, sadistically deformed and crude as Bacon's images were, they always suggested a preoccupation with one of the big problems facing postwar artists: what to do with the human figure. Bacon milled it through glamorous techniques learned from the movies (which Munch had already hinted at) and disembodied it and put it in plastic boxes, but he never tried to get rid of it.

This simultaneous development of an ironic figurative symbolism in Bacon, the Cobra painters or Dubuffet is one more instance in postwar Europe of sharply varied approaches reaching similar results.

12 : The Fate of the Figure in New European Painting

CERTAINLY the somber postwar mood that brought about the grim speculations of Sartre and Camus, and saw the idea of "commitment" gain ground among the poets, was reflected in the "new" painting. A few cultural historians have already noticed the Existentialism seems to have accompanied two differing ideas in postwar European painting:

The first is a heightened, sometimes macabre figurative idiom in which the irony of modern man's position and his tragedy are alluded to directly in the imagery. The cult of the absurd is often celebrated in this branch of postwar art, which would include Dubuffet and the people he influenced, the Cobra painters and a large number of sculptors who favor images of the human figure in decomposition.

The second is the transcendental abstraction called informal, or lyrical, or warm (as opposed to the "cold" abstraction stemming from de Stijl). In this second concept, the artist believes he must go beyond the limitations of perceived nature and defy the inertia of matter. He seeks to transcend the object, divest himself of the weights of matter, mass and all externals that register only in the senses. Since, according to many of these artists, the reality the painter confronts today becomes less and less material, it follows that the "content" of contemporary informal art is precisely this new, nonmaterial reality.

The clear bifurcation these two concepts represent is marked in Europe. In the United States, few forceful artists have explored the figurative aspects of modern painting. When they do, they frequently slip into orthodox expressionism. It is precisely in this area, as I shall try to indicate later, that significant differences between European and American art occur.

Probably the estrangement of poets, philosophers and artists in the United States has a lot to do with the absence of direct allusion to existential problems in most important American art. The only area where direct allusion regularly occurs is in the neo-Dada assemblages where young American painter-sculptors often spell out their indignation quite literally.

In Europe, particularly in the years immediately after the war, there was considerable interchange between artists and writers, and avowed mutual influence. Café life — the most obvious ground for community — continued to stimulate meetings and conversations among practitioners in all the arts as before the war. Particularly important was the re-establishment of old friendships between avant-garde poets and writers and visual artists. Not a few of the significant European contemporary artists intention-ally exposed their ideas to literary colleagues and shaped their thoughts in direct collaboration.

The artist who developed in the clearest parallel to his poetic contemporaries in France was Alberto Giacometti. His figurative sculpture and painting are direct embodi-ments of existential theory. I have no doubt that Giaco-metti's spectral figures "arrived" as he often says, from an unaccountable source, and independent of his many con-versations with the poets. But Giacometti is a very good example of the European artist working in close concert with contemporary poets, building upon an established philosophic base. His image has reverberated, and many American artists have been moved by it, understanding that it represents the other side of the abstract expres-sionist coin.

Giacometti's figures seem disastrously exposed, but they are in fact protected by their very structure — the bone-thin unity from which nothing more could be taken away. Try as it might, the world, the *ambiance* these verticals inhabit, can wear away no more. The figures stand, a throng of ideas, immobile, attendant, suggesting the ab-solute immutability that brings them intact from the far reaches of human history.

The supernatural tension in a gathering of Giacomet-ti's works is generated by a paradox. The contracted fig-ures, standing in proximity to each other, seem to exist by virtue of their neighbors. And yet, never has an artist more directly expressed the ultimate isolation of a human life. Here is the philosophical — existentialist, that is — paradox: Man exists always in a situation, and yet, another entity, *his own life,* stands in relief, alone.

It is no coincidence that Giacometti's work is admired and understood by the postwar literary generation personifying the existentialist sensibility. The symbols of alienation found in Giacometti are also found in Sartre, Camus and Genet, all of whom admire his work. Giacometti's hermetic women, standing on a broad field — the large plaza he often indicates — are comparable to the cloaked Arabs, black against the sun, who form Camus's *royaume* and who give the sense of "immense solitudes" that haunt Camus. Or they are like the cruelly entrapped women, the compressed symbols of circumstantial despair, who motivate Genet's plays. By creating an *ambiance* of isolation, Giacometti reinforces the natural human sense of existing within a situation, or space. We "see" the others. We do not collide with them, or blunder in their tracks — we know they exist in the very space in which we exist. Yet, they can never know our inner being, nor can they die for us.

Since his surrealist days, Giacometti's will was to transcend the familiar facts of human existence. He wrote poetry in which the words were released from normal designations and winged away from the weight of object, people and fact associated with them. His surrealist sculptures were diagrams of fantasy saturated with the feeling of suspension from the vicissitudes of everyday life. He

ALBERTO GIACOMETTI, *Portrait of Diego,* 1957. Oil, 32 x 25½.

(Sidney Janis Gallery, New York)

strived to reduce everything — form and fact — to its spiritual essence.

He sought to do the same in the postwar figures. His demon eliminates and eliminates, and tries, indeed, to erase everything. Still something always remains: the essential core of the personage *taking his place in space.* The tendency to erasure, to deranging the regular human image in order to heighten its existence, appeared in other artists in France, also in England in the work of Francis Bacon, and in the United States in the work of Willem de Kooning, whose impulse was similar in his tense "Woman" series.

Erasure, disintegration of known forms and destruction of the familiar characterize the work of two other French artists who have often been cited as crucial in the emergence of the informal movement: Jean Dubuffet and Jean Fautrier. Both made their forceful sallies immediately after the war, and both found support among poets and painters eager to acknowledge a "new" attitude. Both, furthermore, were ironists whose mood coincided with the moods of such writers as Francis Ponge, Jean Paulhan, Paul Eluard, and others.

Dubuffet is a witty writer and his notes on his own work are illuminating. "Art and pleasantry — there is common blood between these two orders. The unknown, the unprecedented is their common domain." [1] He praised the stories of Poe, the *Chants de Maldoror,* the statues on Easter Island, and exclaimed: "No art without intoxication [*ivresse*]! But then, wild intoxication! Let reason teeter! Delirium! The highest degree of delirium! . . . Art must make one laugh a little, and give one fear a little. Everything, but not bore."

Yet Dubuffet, for all his efforts to mask the finesse of the professional artist in himself, and for all his hearty disdain for elegance and aestheticism, is a *bourgeois peintre malgré lui.*

Unlike many twentieth-century painters, Dubuffet consciously assumed a position. He summed up his predilections, sorted out his convictions, and painted. But he also wrote. And he wrote persuasively, casting far less dust in the eyes than is generally assumed. He wrote that he abhorred the "maniacs," the "snobs" and the "initiates" who frequent art galleries. He said in a thousand different ways that his own art was designated for the "man in the street." He longed for an art that "doesn't know its name." He reminded his audience that everything has its source: that colors come from minerals in the earth, oil from plants, and turpentine from the pine tree.

He explained, often in witty metaphor, that painting is a real language and, in a small essay, "Man Writes on the Sand," indicated a vivid sense of history: "Only the contemporaries of the painter, and even among them only his closest friends, can decipher all the stirring of allusions, and the ellipses that animate the work. It makes no sense except as it functions within the collective humor of the moment in which it was produced."

It is one of the paradoxes that always pursue a man like Dubuffet that the very "snobs" and "aesthetes" he wished to alienate are his most ardent admirers. And it is doubtful if the man on the street, the servant girl, or the many proletarian enthusiasts of Maurice Chevalier — who Dubuffet says created a language superior to that of opera singers — have found Dubuffet's elementary language intelligible.

He claims he has been misread as a satirist. "My position is exclusively that of celebration," he wrote, taking exception to those who saw in him the sophisticated buffoon. (But even an earnest man can't help noticing things, and Dubuffet's total denial of satire and buffoonery is not acceptable.)

While Dubuffet is a bristling, peculiar personality whom André Pieyre de Mandiargues describes as a man "who never leaves his admirers in peace and doesn't always spare his friends," [2] there is a thread of desperate, old-fashioned sincerity in his writings and much in his paintings that brings home the irony of his bourgeois acceptance.

Dubuffet's concern with simplicity, his fundamental back-to-the-earth philosophy, his need to "see" commonplace objects, gestures, human equipment, and above all his uncanny ability to evoke sources (the "territories of origins") have placed him in a leading relationship to other postwar artists. He is particularly close to contemporary poets who, like him, have burned their aesthetic bridges. Typical is the poet Francis Ponge, who with his exacting verbal magnifying glass has examined elements — earth, vegetable, insect and animal life — with the same painstaking super-realism Dubuffet uses. Both artists follow the twentieth-century line of disruption of previous forms; both deny abstraction, and both paradoxically transform their materials to the point of abstraction.

Ponge's poems, often written in prose, come so close to
describing Dubuffet's paintings, and vice versa, that it is
worth quoting segments to show that in France there is an
authentic tie between the two arts.

In "The Three Shops" Ponge writes:

Near the Place Maubert, at the spot where every morning
early I wait for the bus, are three neighbouring shops: a jewel-
ler's, a wood and coal merchant's, a butcher's. Gazing at them
in turn, I observe the behaviour, different in my eyes, of metal,
precious stones, coal, faggots, pieces of meat.

Let us not stop too long over the metals, which are only the
result of a violent or divisive action by man on muds or certain agglomerates. . . .

As to the meat, a trembling at the sight of it, a kind of hor-
ror or sympathy compels me to the greatest discretion. . . .

But the contemplation of wood and coal is a source of joys
as easy as certain and sober which I should be glad to share
. . . I am confining myself to suggesting to you this theme
for meditation 1) TIME OCCUPIED IN VECTORS AL-
WAYS AVENGES ITSELF, BY DEATH. 2) BROWN,
BECAUSE BROWN IS BETWEEN GREEN AND BLACK
ON THE ROAD TO CARBONIZATION, WOOD'S DES-
TINY ALSO INCLUDES — THOUGH TO A MINIMUM
— A GEST, THAT IS ERROR, BLUNDERING, AND ALL
POSSIBLE MISUNDERSTANDINGS.

Dubuffet's elliptical, ambiguous language resembles
even more the language of a poet like Max Jacob.
Jacob also took the "embryonic, the imperfect, the rough
diamonds" that Dubuffet says he loves best, and made of
them the maddening and fascinating equivocal poetic
style of prewar Paris. Puns, solecisms, dirt, toads — the

stuff of Jacob's poetry and Dubuffet's paintings — are tumbled together in what amounts to a passionate quest for truth.

Both men strain to "see" the ordinary in a vision that is potentially extraordinary. Jacob did it when he watched the passers-by on the rue Ravignan and assigned to them mythic roles — Ulysses, Agamemnon *et al*. Dubuffet has consistently tried to duplicate this concentrating staring process — staring until hallucination — in his paintings of people in subways, cows, Arabs and nabobs, landscapes, tables, earth (though characteristically, Dubuffet denies that he looks very closely).

Burlesque, which Dubuffet feels has been overstressed, is nevertheless one of the most valuable elements in his work. Like Jacob, who Marcel Raymond said was in the tradition of the seventeenth-century masters of travesty, Dubuffet *has* made fun of the *pompiers* in painting and of their outmoded clichés. His own relationship to the early French "macaronic" poets can be taken as the same as Jacob's. In this connection, Raymond cites an extremely interesting passage from Bernard Fontenelle's *Dialogue des Morts:*

Oh I see that you have not understood the perfection of jesting. It contains all Wisdom. One can find absurdity, in everything . . . I transposed the divine Aeneid of your Virgil into burlesque verse, and there is no better way of showing that the magnificent and the ridiculous are so close that they touch each other. Everything resembles those tricks of perspective in which figures scattered here and there form, for in-

stance an emperor if you look at them from a certain angle; if
you change your angle, the same figures represent a beggar.[3]

Circuitous as Dubuffet's or Jacob's or Ponge's route may
be, they all reflect a romantic nostalgia for simplicity, albeit simplicity seen through the facets of irony, and they
all share what might be called a faith that in the commonplace even the sophisticated man may find salvation.

Dubuffet's language, like any poet's, can be discussed
from many vantage points. It hangs together as a complex
mass of nouns of his materials — the plaster, ordure,
whitewash, stones and varnish — punctuated by such a
wide inventory of other parts of speech (whirling, zigzagging or flaccid lines for verbs; dots, colors, tones for adjec-
tives and so on) that it is quite hopeless to classify.

It is a language that leans heavily and unabashedly on
the vernacular — which is to say that it is full of repeti-
tions and intentional clichés. The thousands — literally
thousands — of works Dubuffet has produced since the
war have gone raging around the world with unbraked
momentum. An adoring public is led willingly through
the dusty tundras and swarming animistic mud of his
world. Dubuffet inundates us with images using the hit-
'em-hard technique of contemporary advertising as no
other artist has done. By virtue of his implacable energy,
he manages to keep his images alive and to give a wry
twist to a technique usually reserved for commerce.

His impact on younger painters is inestimable, from the
first 1945 and 1946 exhibitions to the present. In 1946,
Dubuffet's *succès de scandale* caught the attention of the

young in Paris. Dubuffet's experiments with materials — the thick matrices of mudlike consistency, the built-up textures which he called "unform" — made a profound impression on those who were only too happy to let reason teeter and find the archaistic truth Dubuffet obliquely and ironically postulated. He inspired them to explore the ridiculous, to understand, through their work, the absurdities of the human condition.

Dubuffet's attitude in many ways reflects his malevolent affection for the trickery that delighted the Dadaists. He is quite capable of saying divergent things and holding them both as true. And capable also of denying everything he has ever said.

His protestations of earnestness are often tongue-in-cheek. Whether "Mirobolus, Macadam et Cie/Hautes Pâtes," the scandalous exhibition of May 1946, was really intended to have a detergent effect on French art remains an open question. In 1945 Dubuffet had begun his collection of what he called *L'Art Brut,* but with characteristic craftiness, he didn't display it until 1949, after he had already shown his own *art brut.* In his statement of definition, Dubuffet said that the works were done by people uncontaminated by artistic culture, namely inmates of mental institutions, children and authentic primitives. "We witness here the artistic process in all its purity, raw, reinvented on all its levels by the maker."

As the exhibition of *L'Art Brut* proved, Dubuffet had drawn heavily on his collection for inspiration, often repeating practically unchanged the motifs he found. Whether he really regarded himself as "uncontaminated

JEAN DUBUFFET, *Portrait of Jean Paulhan with a Lion's Mane,* 1946. Oil, 43½ x 35½.

(*Collection of Mr. and Mrs. Arnold H. Maremont*)

by artistic culture" in these reiterations of deranged images is an open question. What is certain, however, is that
Dubuffet's diabolic energy invested in this enterprise was
transformed by hundreds of other artists into earnest works
that they regarded as works of art.

The other painter whose exhibition immediately after
the war scandalized the critics and therefore drew the attention of the young was Jean Fautrier. To my mind Fautrier remains a minor painter whose obsessive reiterations,
contrary to those of Dubuffet, lack vitality. But as a cata-
lyst, Fautrier functioned. His role in the unfolding of the
European avant-garde, while it is not nearly as important
as his enthusiasts claim, is nevertheless legitimately under-
lined in recent art history.

Like Dubuffet, Fautrier was concerned with matter itself and the problem of transforming its inertia. His thick,
pastrylike surfaces excited the younger generation, already
searching for unorthodox materials and means. In his work
they saw a larger pattern of disintegration, of atomization,
of deliberate destruction of given patterns of vision and association. It was the way he built up his material into
thick-textured objects which impressed them — quite differently from the way André Malraux was impressed.[4]

For him, Fautrier is "one of the few contemporary painters who owes nothing to anyone." No doubt Fautrier's first
show after the war, with its grim title, "Hostages," and its
horrifying exploration of a wartime theme, communicated
with Malraux's literary mind. Michel Ragon writes that "it
is not by mere chance that his 'writers' bear the names of
Jean Paulhan, Francis Ponge, René de Solier. They are
three authors having the same tendency to delousing, to

scratching, to the edging approach, to clawing, to grubbing,
to stirring the paste of words in the Dresden china cup."
Fautrier's appeal to Malraux, on the other hand, comes
from his tragic or pathetic side, according to Ragon. "Malraux sees the slayer of beasts, the witness of the Hostages,
the misanthropist of the Vallée aux Loups, the seeker of
whom some say that he has sacrificed his talent for an aber-
ration, like Uccello, or the hero of Balzac's 'Unknown
Masterpiece.'" Paulhan characterized Fautrier's painting
as a "world that is excessive and monstrous, violent and,
as it were, abusive." The obsessive qualities seen in Fautrier's need to repeat the same images in extensive series
(distorted heads, boxes, buttocks, glasses, etc.) appealed to
artists whose conflicts between that which is unique and
that which is mass-produced became unbearable.

Giacometti, Dubuffet, Fautrier and a number of others
began with the human figure and the events in which it
participated. What happened to the physiological entity of
man in the course of their imaginative explorations became in its turn a subject of the work of art. Neither purely
subjective nor purely objective, the imagery these artists
put forward was intended to suggest the supreme difficulty
in assessing "reality." In this, these artists can be said to
have grappled with existentialist theory, lingering long
and thoughtfully over the problem of the "concrete" experience as opposed to abstract experience, which, in its
way, is just as real. That the tangible event is still evident
in their work distinguishes it from the work of lyrical abstractionists whose effort has been to transcend object and
event in the everyday world.

13 : Transcendental Abstraction

THE TENDENCY toward unequivocal abstraction — a romantic lyricism that strains beyond the limits of perceived nature — is more pronounced today than ever before. Lyrical abstractionists stemmed from many traditions, often sharply divergent traditions such as cubism and surrealism, but they all arrived at a point where they willingly bypassed the material presence of the human in the hope of presenting the new reality they sensed: the reality of dematerialized nature. Most of the "warm" lyricists, or tachistes, or abstract expressionists, do not feel the check of existential doubt in the same way as Dubuffet or Giacometti. Their vision of nature has undergone a radical change.

Artists have always speculated about their relationship to nature. In general, the artist has never had a static or "exact" relationship to nature even if he claimed to, for it

is in the very effort to understand nature — never wholly
rewarded — that art is created. At all times, probably, there have been temperaments given to transcendental abstraction and others to whom the conflict between direct observation and imagination has become itself the subject of their art (this being the case with Giacometti, for instance). In certain periods one or another tendency has been pronounced. The contemporary period is weighted in favor of transcendental abstraction.

In the history of European art the emphasis shifts again and again. The medieval artist whose guiding principle was *universalia sunt realia* was prepared to move far from "observed reality." The Renaissance painter, however, was excited by the so-called scientific spirit, and had faith in the observable, material world. Leon Battista Alberti insisted that "that which cannot be seized with the eye has absolutely nothing to do with the painter." Alberti and his contemporaries accepted the Aristotelian notion of art as imitation. Yet, in the sixteenth century, there were strange imaginative digressions from orderly Renaissance thought, and even Dürer remarked that though art stands firmly fixed in nature, "who can rend her from there, he only possesses her." By suggesting that the artist "rends" his art from nature Dürer does not conform to the simple imitative theory but brings the selective spirit of the artist into play.

A century later Poussin suggests that "Art is not a different thing from nature nor can it pass beyond nature's boundaries. For that light of knowledge which by natural gift is scattered here and there appears in different men at different times and places and is collected into one body by art . . ." With this statement, Poussin places the artist *within* nature.

Add to Poussin's statement that of Goya in his introduction to the "Caprichos" in which he said that he had not found it possible to copy nature, that departing from her entirely he was "obliged to exhibit to the eye forms and attitudes which hitherto had existed only in the human mind . . ."

The nineteenth century began the final work of placing the artist *within* nature and the twentieth century completed the job. Romanticists such as Coleridge deliberately turned attention away from conventional "observed reality" toward the universal. "The artist must imitate that which is within the thing, that which is active through form and figure and discourses to us by symbols — the *Naturgeist,* or spirit of nature."

More extreme idealists such as the painter Caspar David Friedrich already in the early years of the nineteenth century passed even beyond the *Naturgeist:* "The true, the only source of art is our heart, the language of a pure and candid soul . . . Close your physical eye in order to see your canvas with the eye of the spirit. Then, bring to the light of day that which you have seen in your night in order that its action works on other beings, from the exterior to the interior."

Teodor de Wyzewa said in 1886 that art "must recreate, in full consciousness, and by means of signs, the total life of the universe, that is to say, of the soul where the varied dream we call the universe is played."

The romantic movement pressed on and on, seeking always to abolish the barrier between that which is observed
and the observer. The whole symbolist movement pointed
to the ultimate dissolution of the firm boundaries inherited
from the Renaissance and to a transcendental abstraction
in which the artist immerses himself in the universe and
records the "signs" of his experiences there.

In European painting, the surrealism of Miró and Arp,
in which forms rationalized from observed nature become
an independent alphabet, and in which the inner energy of
the forms themselves is universal rather than particular in
significance, led directly into contemporary lyrical abstraction. Paul Klee's preoccupation with cosmic symbology as
well as Kandinsky's legacy — the need to affirm a possibly
pure art of abstraction — all this is a fulfillment of romantic prophecy.

Contemporary painting steps out, even beyond the idealism of the nineteenth-century romantics. For the contemporary lyricist, form is not only a manifestation of his interior
condition, not only a "correspondence" with the visible
and invisible symbols of this world, but an expression of a
new reality confirmed by philosophical speculation of very
recent date.

This new reality, called "other" by the tachistes, has
been discussed more and more in the European art press.
Historians have already traced its manifestation in painting.
Histories of the "informal" movement in France name
several seminal figures, among them two Germans who
became identified with the School of Paris before the war
— Wols and Hartung.

Wols (Alfred Otto Wolfgang Schulze) had spent a year at the Bauhaus in 1931 before coming to Paris. His visionary temperament was evidently nourished and deeply affected by his contact with Paul Klee. When he arrived in Paris, he found his spiritual home among the surrealist poets. Wols's paintings then were spidery, pale little watercolors crowded with nightmarish symbols: wall-fortress towns floating in menacing seas, plasmic figures garroted, metamorphosing human organs exposed to whirlwinds. Though parts of this unsettling lexicon of symbols were shared by other surrealist painters, Wols's work seemed to come from another tradition — the tradition of the wild visions that arrive in works of Bosch, Redon, Bresdin and Ensor.

In 1941 while Wols was in Marseilles hiding from the Nazis, Kay Boyle became his friend and wrote later: "When Wols walked toward you through the hot sunlight of the Midi you saw blazing in his eyes the fire that raged within him."

A frequent symbol in his paintings at that time was a sailing vessel trying to escape from the malaise of those horror-ridden cities Wols dreamed in his work.

His melancholy was reflected in the choice of the authors he illustrated before his death in 1951, Artaud, Kafka and Sartre among them. His was the art of a haunted, thoroughly lacerated spirit, and his legend in Paris today has much in common with Pollock's in New York.

Toward the end of the war, Wols painted the abstractions that established him as an "informal." These canvases were never very large, but they compressed a vision

WOLS (Alfred Otto Wolfgang Schulze), *Number 14,* c. 1942. Gouache, 10⅚16 x 14¾.

(Grace Borgenicht Brandt)

of a dark, moiled, oneiric cosmos in which flying orbs were sucked into vertical abysses and light lashed out from hidden depths in the picture. His use of coiled spirals and tangles of line overriding his images was incidental to the manipulation of his paint, often handled with classical restraint in spite of the vaulting imagery.

The lyrical, romantic impulse in Wols, which found its answering voices in postwar France, has become increasingly important to young French painters. His view of the imagination, close to views of American painters, speaks intimately to them:

Everything that I dream occurs in a very large and very beautiful unknown city with vast suburbs and seas, I don't dare to draw it. At each instant, in each thing, eternity is there. Words are chameleons, music has the right to be abstract, the experience that nothing is explicable leads to the dream, explain music not, explain dreams not, the unseizable penetrates everything, it is necessary to know that everything rhymes.[1]

Around 1947 and 1948, Wols was painting his most intense visions, and all of Paris was saturated with Existentialist discussions. Perhaps the idea that being, authentic being, lies on the other side of despair engaged him. Perhaps the notion that a man must travel to the depths of hopelessness, which is the realm of the absurd, before he can know the integrity of his existence meant something to him. In any case, he seemed to emerge from depression with the hope that, indeed, "everything rhymes" in the universe. Because of this faith, a number of critics have suggested that Wols was concerned with a Taoist vision of unity.

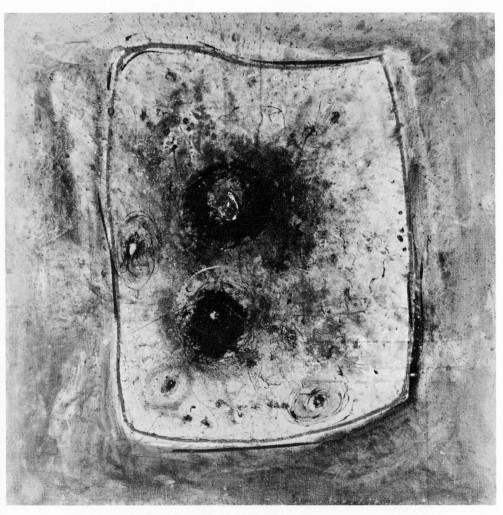

WOLS (Alfred Otto Wolfgang Schulze), *Painting*. Oil, $31\frac{7}{8}$ x 32.

(*The Museum of Modern Art, New York; Mr. and Mrs. John de Menil Fund*)

Wols's unified image was expressed most fully then in his small watercolors. He worked with pale melting tones of red, blue and yellow, barely tinting the page. Within the liquid continuity of these thin washes he painted, or drew with ink, shapes of roots, insects, thorns, blood vessels and capsules that were always intricately intertwined. Quite often a pale sphere — the moon or sun — was integrated in these compositions. It was seen as a part of the whole, the microcosm that Wols dreamed. Each of these small water colors had a "heart," a center from which all events and forms radiated.

Wols's transcendentalism with its emphasis on that which cannot be explained in words, on a world revealed only in dreams, was welcome in 1947, when the established conventions in painting seemed impossible to carry on. Moreover, Wols was handing on a principle that had been submerged — at least in France — for a number of years after Kandinsky had established it: the right of painting, like music, to be abstract. Since the symbolist movement, with its explorations of synesthesia, its acknowledgment of ambiguity as a tool in the hands of an artist, this defense of painting in terms of music has been renewed with force and urgency.

Hans Hartung, too, insisted on the right of painting to be free from all binding literal reference. His impulse to abstraction occurred very early and his work of the mid-thirties demonstrates that he had been doing tachiste or informal painting long before the others.

Hartung is a purist, and in a sense, is closer to Mondrian in his search for absolute universals than he is to the emotive abstract expressionists. His paintings are composed of "strokes," as he has said, that in their curve-versus-angle relationships are intended to symbolize the unseen movements in the cycles of nature. He has reduced and reduced in recent years until a painting or drawing is sometimes composed of a single "sign" riding in a void. His tendency to rely on the single expressive line to divide and qualify the picture space has made its mark on many younger painters, as has his preference for line. Hartung's work has been discussed in relation to Oriental calligraphy, but he has pointed out that the Orient is far from his thoughts. His relationship to music, however, is acknowledged, and he is reported to use music as he works.

In the years following the war, many School of Paris painters converged in a lyrical abstraction that seemed inevitably, historically necessary. Even so surrealistically inclined a painter as Vieira da Silva was pulled irresistibly toward the cryptic plastic language of signs, creating a webby, delicately stressed all-over space rather than the deep vistas for which she first became noted.

Another influential painter whose evolution toward lyrical abstraction is marked by natural inevitability is Pierre Tal-Coat. Born in 1905, son of a Breton fisherman, Tal-Coat arrived in 1925 in Paris, where he accepted the prevailing Picasso-drenched aesthetic. His work was fundamentally figurative for years, with certain stylistic concessions to the flattening and foreshortening of form instituted in the synthetic cubist days. Yet even so patient and slow a painter as Tal-Coat, whose formation was definitely within the boundaries of orthodox figuration, succumbed to an overwhelming new form-will. The hallowed modern traditions of prewar France simply could not survive after 1945.

Tal-Coat's relationship to nature shows the typical change over the years from his being an observer to being a part of the thing observed. When Georges Duthuit wrote about his work, he jumped into extreme abstraction: "Let's not be afraid of words: it is a matter of metaphysical painting." But is this man who painted for years in Cézanne country, who to this day rambles about the countryside squinting with intense concentration at "nature," studying a landscape he knows by heart — is he really a metaphysician?

Like Cézanne, he has meditated on his experiences in nature with a patience that knows no bounds. He is not so much a metaphysician as a man who has intuitively grasped a new reality and understood it through his own physical and spiritual experience. Over the years he has ruminated until, to him, the wind itself is as tangible as the bread he breaks in the morning. He arrives at his "cosmic" painting not so much through metaphysical speculation as through the sturdy realism that makes a man stroll in the dusk observing with perpetual interest how birds flee from his shadow.

Shadows, at a certain point, became tangibilia to Tal-Coat. Sometime around 1950 the ground line disappeared permanently from his work. Signs, sketched in wispy charcoal and then floated in yellow-ocher atmosphere, became universalizing motifs. That is, they signified trees, shadows, birds, movement all at once.

Toward 1956 he began a series of leaping figures —

PIERRE TAL-COAT, *Le Saut IV,* 1955-1956. Oil, 9½ x 13.

(Galerie Maeght)

innocent stick figures vaulting into a void, completely foreign to the terra firma of his prewar landscapes. The jumping figures were after all only signs, however, for substance and shadow were rendered in the same flurried, vague way. With the empathy of an Oriental, Tal-Coat vaulted himself, his feelings, his substance into those floating shadows. The leap was the movement of the elements, no different from the take-off of birds, the sway of trees, footsteps in spring fields, movement of flocks and contour of rocks, all of which he subsequently incorporated as motifs in his paintings. The images were images of Tal-Coat simultaneously inhabiting and observing space.

In his most recent work, Tal-Coat's signs no longer signify directly. They are stenographic marks that, spelled out by the eye, form a unity. His impulse to abstraction dominates his eye and hand, and there is no turning back. Tal-Coat represents, in this sense, an irreversible direction in modern art, and has been followed to the vague and vast places by many young Parisian painters, just as Tobey, Kline and Rothko were followed by the young in the early 1950's in the United States.

III : Speculations

14 : Irony in Modern Art

THE DISTINGUISHING characteristic of the most re-
nowned contemporary European artists — Giacometti and
Dubuffet for instance — is their irony. Broadly speaking,
the difference between postwar art in Europe and the
United States is that most Europeans cannot help being
ironic, while most Americans cannot help lacking irony.

The quality of irony is not easily defined. I use the term
in a flexible, deliberately equivocal sense in order to suggest a mood, a state of mind, a *Zeitgeist*. To enter my speculative definition one would have to accept as a basic premise
that style is the man and that his mood, qualified by events,
reflection and temperament, is registered in his work.

The word "irony" derives from the Greek word *eiron*.
In its simple definition, the *eiron* is a man who dissembles.
In Aristotelian terms, he is a man who deprecates himself.

Socrates deprecated himself, pretended to know nothing, in order to use his ironic questioning technique.

In literature the term "irony," according to Northrup Frye, indicates a technique of appearing to be less than one is.[1] It becomes a technique of saying as little and meaning as much as possible. Or, in a more general way, it is a pattern of words that turns away from direct statement or its own obvious meaning. Another definition holds that irony constitutes the degree of difference between what is expected and what is said.

It is not difficult to move into the visual arts from these definitions. The technique of saying little and meaning much translated into painting appears in early cubist collages in which bits of string, paper and simulated wood were assembled in patterns that the artist intended to move away from direct statement. Picasso knows the value of paper and string, but by pretending he does not, he invests them with a different value. When Kurt Schwitters perfected his "Merz" collages, he used railway tickets and brand-name labels with ironic innocence.

Schwitters did not say to the viewer: Look, here are bits of everyday life, a ticket which can be used on a train, a label from a Kirsch bottle that is no longer full, a postage stamp, and that is all they are. Rather, he pointed to them, pretended that is what they were, but wished to express something quite different. He endowed them with values that in themselves they do not have.

Schwitters was a Dadaist and Dada was an ironic movement above all. Active between 1916 and 1923 roughly, the Dadas, like the Futurists, intended to sweep away aesthetic pretention; to purge "Art" of its bourgeois complicity and, ironically, to restore it to the dignity seemingly lost in the social and political unrest of the period. Although the method of combat they developed was derision, the end they worked toward was its opposite. Schwitters, for instance, sought to "lead art back to life" and to find a "universal expression for all men." If Schwitters collected the throwaways of daily existence and assembled them in compositions that seemed absurd to his viewers at the time, he did so with irony. Ultimately the "meaning" with which he invested his collages by such indirect methods is recognized.

In Frye's analysis of fiction, classified according to the hero's power of action, a novel is ironic if the hero is inferior in power or intelligence so that we have "a sense of looking down at a scene of bondage, frustration or absurdity." There is a victim chosen at random. Nothing he has done warrants catastrophe that overcomes him, and the reasons for catastrophe are absurdly inadequate. Nineteenth-century European literature, particularly French literature, is saturated with ironic elements of this sort. Precursors to the symbolist movement, such as Alfred de Vigny and Gérard de Nerval, express the tragic isolation of the ironic hero, with his frustration and sense of abandonment. There is a remarkable passage in Alfred de Vigny's 1824 journal in which he prefigures Kafka, the ironist par excellence:

Here is human life.
I imagine a crowd of men, women and children wrapt in a profound sleep. They awaken imprisoned, they accustom them-

selves to their prison and make little gardens. Little by little, they notice that one after another, they are being removed forever. They know neither why they are in prison, nor where they are taken afterwards, and they know that they will never know.

Nevertheless, there are among them those who never cease arguing in order to know the history of their trial, and there are those who invent the dramas; others who tell what becomes of them after the prison without really knowing.

Are they not mad?

It is certain that the master of the prison, the governor, would have let us know if he had wanted to, both about our arrest and our trial. . . . *We are not sure of knowing everything when we leave the dungeon, but we are sure of not knowing anything within.*

A similar mood of ironic frustration moved Gérard de Nerval. In *El Desdichado* he characterizes himself as "the dark man, the inconsolable widower, the Prince of Aquitania whose tower has been torn down." In what was probably intended as his own *Epitaph,* he wrote: "He wished to know all things but discovered nothing. And when the moment came when, tired of this life, one winter evening at last his soul was torn from him, he went away asking, Why did I come?"

Ironic elements became more and more frequent in French literature toward the end of the nineteenth century, and have decidedly dominated the twentieth century. Think of the preoccupation with Hamletism from Jules Laforgue to Max Jacob to Paul Valéry. And consider the wide influence of Kafka, who above all other twentieth-century writers gives us the powerless hero, the victim of unmotivated disaster. He pretends that he knows nothing about it, that even he, the writer, has been chosen at random. Beckett more recently has burrowed deep in the ironic mode, stringing up long sequences of random detail. His "hero" perfectly conveys what Frye calls the sense of looking down on a scene of bondage, frustration or absurdity. The ultimate note in European literary irony occurs in recent French novels where the hero is altogether dissolved. The authors substitute the absurdity of obscurely related concrete objects for the absurdity of exterior fate. These authors (among them Natalie Sarraute and Michel Butor) have deprecated themselves to the limit, surpassing even Frye's definition.

The ironic or self-deprecating European visual artist, like his literary contemporaries, pretends to know nothing, either about the world or himself. But he only pretends. The American artist on the whole does not pretend. He really believes in Montaigne's attitude of *que sais-je;* really believes that through his work he will discover something about himself and the world. The European tends to think less of discovering than of revealing. Picasso: An artist doesn't seek, he finds.

In Europe the arts were more directly shaped by the postwar consciousness of the random element in personal and communal tragedy. With Camus exasperation appears in a high sober tone of tragic irony. In Ionesco it is a comic intoning, a piling up of commonplaces, a sardonic, absolute, absurd outcry. Europeans are specialists in ferreting out the uncomfortable ironies of the human condition.

Consider Dubuffet in this context. No one could be more consistently ironic. Yet, beneath his pleasantries is the exasperated, realistic, melancholy artist who tried after the war to set up conditions in which he could work. He managed to sweep the absurdities of the past out of his ken only to be confronted with the absurdities of the present. His ironic method of coping with them was to pretend he knew nothing. His desire to know nothing is obvious in the 1943 drawings of stick-figure children, subways and cities outlined and colored as if by a seven-year-old.

By deliberately deprecating himself — which is to say European culture — Dubuffet did make certain revelations. He wrote: "I have always loved to work only in the most common materials, those which one doesn't think of at first because they are too common and close and seem to us improper. I like to proclaim that my art is an enterprise of rehabilitation of degraded values. The voice of the dust, the soul of the dust — they interest me many times more than the flower, the tree or the horse."

But even the soul of the dust is expressed ironically. One of the significant aspects of irony in modern art is its ultimate detachment, a philosophic and psychological distance which precludes didacticism and moralizing. What Dubuffet is saying when he paints an ungainly woman, her bloated body splayed, her essence described as a mass of thickening mud, is: You have never noticed how alike we humans are, how nearly like the mud from which zoologists say we have come, how primitive and undifferentiated we really are. He knows this is not the whole story, but must exaggerate and generalize in order to show the disparity between what is thought and what is. The work is ironic in the dissembling attitude of its author, in its detachment, in its tragicomic symbolization of alienation.

Dubuffet's powerful portraits, in which oversized faces are tracked and troughed to suggest the terrain of a rocky landscape, again stress irony, showing the disparity between what is expected and what is. All these personages are given names, mostly of famous poets Dubuffet has known, but their faces are intended to be anonymous, craggy testimonies of the common clay from which we all spring. A great poet? No, says Dubuffet, just another agglomeration of particles.

Dubuffet's overt ironies, as when he paints a picture called "Businessmen's Lunch" and makes it look like a Last Supper, or when he follows his strong writing impulse and paints critical comments and dirty words into the conventional scheme of an oil painting, are not nearly so telling as those he conceals in his series tending toward abstraction. "I am pleased to see life in trouble," he says, implying with supreme confidence that he can put it to rights.

De Kooning's "Woman" series is often compared to Dubuffet's "Corps de Dame" series but is remote from the ironic mood. The very anger implicit in it is foreign to the ironist's detachment. It is romantic and idealistic in the way it strikes out in the full flush of feeling to characterize a detested aspect of human nature. The vital landscape mingles with the woman's figure, and the flesh stridently declares itself at war with the erosive landscape. Because of the directness of statement, and the battling attitude of

JEAN DUBUFFET, *Business Prospers (Le Commerce Prospère)*, 1961. Oil, 65 × 86⅝.

the artist, his anger, the picture pattern does not turn away from its own obvious meaning and is essentially nonironic.

Giacometti, on the other hand, is essentially European in his sense of tragic irony. Even in conversation he adopts the ironic tone. He assured me that the attenuated form of his sculptures was unintentional. "I start out to do a normal, fleshy woman, and this is what comes." Obviously he is endowed with intelligence and superior sensory equipment. He wills to forget what he knows and learns; to pretend that indeed he knows not what he does in order to put into existence his symbols of tragic fate. The irony lies in his use of the human figure: everyone knows what a human figure looks like, he tells us, but this is how it really is when it takes its place in an oppressive universe.

The ironic mood can even be detected in the work of artists who left the human figure behind. Wols was an ironist in a sense that American painters were not. No matter how "cosmic" the content of Wols's informal abstraction was, his work remained in an intimate scale. His knowing sadness, his circumstantial agony, were expressed in ironic scale. That is, eruptive feeling was there but it cohabited with the consciousness in Wols that made him paint the *disparity* between the elevated dream and the chaos of reality. Never the one or the other.

The humiliation and disillusion that followed the Second World War intensified ironic responses. A simple nineteenth-century definition of irony tinged with New World simplicism appears in Alfred North Whitehead's dialogues, where he defines irony as "a depressive frame of mind in people or an age who have lost faith." He regarded

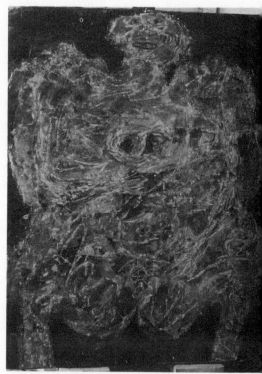

WILLEM DE KOONING,
Woman and Bicycle, 1952-1953. Oil, 76½ x 49.

(*The Whitney Museum of American Art, New York*)

JEAN DUBUFFET, *Court Circuit Bleu,*
Corps de Dame, 1951. Oil, 46 x 35¼.

(*Courtesy of Sidney Janis Gallery, New York*)

irony as decadent and, to some extent, irresponsible. Like
Whitehead, Americans are not geared to irony. Where
Wols would knowingly paint the disparity between dream
and reality, most American painters would not have been
concerned with it. Though they too experienced the loss of
faith, profound revulsion and concomitant depression of
the war, their work became a means of dispelling the
critical ironic attitude.

This is not to say that American painting is the product
of a naïvely optimistic climate. On the contrary, the American painter, lacking a sense of irony, was perhaps more
desperate. He appreciated as much as Dubuffet the necessity of dust and mud to arrive at the "breakthrough." He
experimented with matter itself and minimized his editorial role. But the American painter's despair most often
drove him outward, into spaces where the disparity between dream ideal and actual misery was absorbed by a
countering thrust. He struggled to be free of what he sensed
was an overwhelming — perhaps defeating — burden of
responsibility taken on by the European ironists. In the way
Americans symbolized space — vast, continuous and laby-
rinthine as in Pollock, or boundless, unyielding planes as
in Still — the drive to openness, to the surmounting of
melancholy through mindless passion, anger and exalted
lyricism, is dominant.

In many American paintings catastrophe is there, hovering nearby, but it is held at bay. It remains a probability.
In ironic European counterparts, however, it has come to
pass and the artist has accepted its ravages and integrated
the fragments in his work.

A good example of the nonironic American painter is Clyfford Still. Unlike the true ironist who tends to minimize his role as moralist, giving himself over to the notion of pure art, Still has cultivated a position as keeper of the truth, a prophet.

His utterances are never ironic. He speaks instead with the visionary passion of the puritan. He despises "those who find the aura of death more reassuring than their own impotence or fears." He speaks exaltedly of "the journey that one must make with no respite or short cuts" and does not seem to doubt that he will reach the glory of the "clear air and high and limitless plain." He warns his viewers not to underestimate his work and its power for life.

In his work, the vast dense surfaces are not bounded. The lightning-bolt rents are rude shocks to the eye. His dream of the "truly free vision" is not questioned. He is observing tremendous, powerful phenomena. His statement is direct, its meaning immediately apparent, and one doesn't feel that he is painting any disparity between his dream and his lived reality.

There are, of course, American ironists, though they occur far less frequently than in Europe. Theirs is an oblique irony, a psychological predisposition rather than a sophisticated program.

Philip Guston for instance, has been nurtured as much by the ironic writers of modern times such as Kafka, Valéry and Chekhov as he has by modern painting. His own attitudes, expressed in both his work and his conversation, are distinctly ironic. His quest is for a natural equilibrium which he secretly knows to be nonexistent. He is an *eiron*

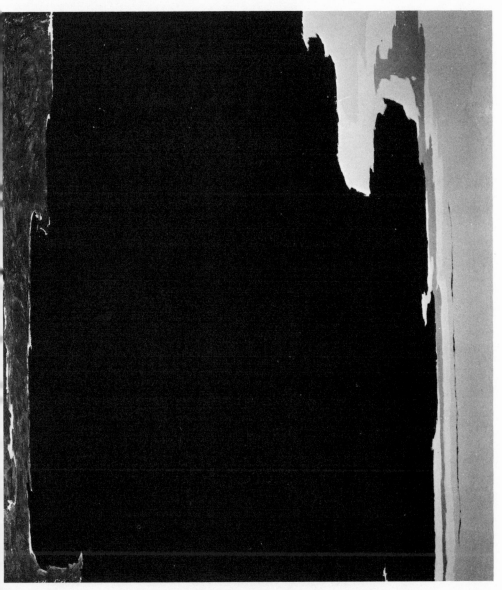

CLYFFORD STILL, *Painting*, 1951. Oil, 94 x 82.

(The Museum of Modern Art, New York; Blanchette Rockefeller Fund)

in that he deprecates his role, pretends not to know, and forgets his painting culture as much as possible in order to reveal. His dialectic approach, in which he always opposes distinct form to indistinct form, rude color to delicate color, movement to stasis, and incorporates all sorts of contradictions, is in itself an ironic mode of apprehending experience.

He has said that he wants to touch the point of emotion that hovers between tears and laughter. Both comic and tragic elements play in recent paintings where shaky structures lumber into the foreground, comically unsure of themselves and threatened by the encroachments of their environment. The teetering and last-minute recovery of balance of these anthropomorphically reminiscent shapes is in itself an ironic statement of the human condition.

Guston's scale is usually not overpowering. He never moves into the boundless spaces that his nonironic colleagues ply. On the contrary, his discourse with the elements of existence is knowing and self-limited. In what appears to be an almost childish perversity of form, Guston clears away memory habits and hackneyed moralizations in order to define the ironies of his own existence.

An obvious irony verging on broad satire appears in the work of neo-Dada painters. Their chief method is juxtaposition of commonplace images which they pretend are not related to one another, but which form a new entity, a new image. Feigned innocence allows them to say one thing and mean another.

In his suite of illustrations for Dante's *Inferno,* Robert Rauschenberg used the ironic technique. In some of the

PHILIP GUSTON, *Duo,* 1961. Oil, 72¼ x 68.

(Sidney Janis Gallery, New York)

illustrations, roaring racing cars appear as such, but they are really intended to be visual equivalents to the demon squads of Dante's thirteenth-century Inferno. The Dante figure itself is ironic. Rauschenberg shows a small impassive man, lined up against a medical measuring chart, his feet pinned to the ground line, his arms pinioned to his sides, his genitals hidden by a towel. Far from being the proud man of destiny Dante conceived himself, Rauschenberg's Dante is peculiarly twentieth century: He is a born victim, a Kafkaesque hero who goes through many fateful experiences but who never seems to be able to discover the significance of them. He stands there a perfect target for Fate. Characteristically in the ironic mode, the indirect statement of Dante brings in its wake further meanings. The Dante before the measuring chart can also be seen as the imperturbable man, the saint who, in fifteenth-century temptation pictures, stares complacently into the distance while demons perform obscenities all around. So certain is he of ultimate grace that he can be impassive.

Ironic elements occur in the imagery of artists whose works touch on the comic or grotesque. We laugh or grimace when we see the amoeboid shapes in Miró's paintings straining toward a kiss. We are laughing not so much at the individual forms but the way in which they act. In them there is an inevitable anthropomorphic return. A Punch and Judy battle, even abstractly posed as it is sometimes in Guston's paintings, suggests the awkward, cruel and imbalanced gestures of ourselves, our thoughts, the way our imaginations labor.

Recent paintings by Robert Motherwell show cumber-

ERRATUM

Due to an unfortunate error the picture by Robert Motherwell entitled *Two Figures with Cerulean Blue Stripe,* which appears on page 189 of this book, was printed upside down. The publisher extends apologies to the artist, to the owner of the picture and to the author of the book.

ROBERT MOTHERWELL, *Two Figures with Cerulean Blue Stripe,* 1960. Oil, 84 x 109.

(Collection of Mr. and Mrs. Carlo Grossman)

some shapes rocking, toddling, staggering. They struggle toward definition. Many of them have vaguely anthropomorphic outlines, though it is as if the human figure were tied in a sack and struggles to be free of it. In the struggle of these forms, pushing and poking out from their center depths, there is a tragic and comic mixture. It is as if the artist were attempting to get inside of form itself to discover its structure and is temporarily ensnared.

"Laughter," said Baudelaire, "is the expression of double or contradictory feelings." Such double or contradictory feelings tend to be ironic.

15 : Expressionism and Motion

IN MANY WAYS Americans have carried out the possibilities suggested by a Russian European, Wassily Kandinsky. He was not a master of irony. On the contrary, he was a romantic idealist whose consciousness of a rhetorical responsibility never left him. The negative criticism implicit in contemporary ironic modes might very well have shocked and repelled Kandinsky. It was his belief, nourished by a nineteenth-century background, that man was the better for art, and could, in fact, help shape the destiny of mankind through his art. Nothing could be less marked by irony than his optimistic treatise *Concerning the Spiritual in Art.*[1]

Kandinsky wanted to "touch under the skin of nature her essence and her content." With romantic intensity he was able to regard the elements he had isolated — the point and line — as beings. In their movements he was able to detect deep, hidden relationships. Kandinsky's faith in "inner necessity" and his ability to envision innumerable possible spaces enabled him to prophesy abstract expressionism:

There is gradually coming into use, as the only possible road to objective form, a more denuded type of construction. It is not obvious geometric configurations that will be the richest in possibilities but hidden ones, emerging unnoticed from the canvas and meant for the soul rather than the eye . . . The hidden construction may be composed of seemingly fortuitous shapes without apparent connection. But the outer presence of such a connection is proof of its inner presence.

The "seemingly fortuitous shapes without apparent connection" that Kandinsky prophesied have become the essence of "informal" or "abstract expressionist" painting. The term "abstract expressionism" was in fact first applied to the art inspired by Kandinsky. Peter Selz found the term in the German art magazine *Der Sturm* in 1919, used to describe painting that "creates objects which are not taken from nature but are related to nature through their rhythm."

When Alfred Barr was lecturing in 1929, and thereafter, on Kandinsky, he reinstated the term, applying it to Kandinsky's early abstract improvisations. Although there was little direct influence of German expressionism on the "new American painting," it is significant that the term "abstract expressionism" was revived around 1946 to describe that painting in America in which "seemingly fortu-itous" shapes appeared.

It is true that there were few exhibitions of German expressionism in the United States. But, as I said earlier, Kandinsky's theories were familiar to a few from 1913 on. If there was no specific German influence, there were a number of striking affinities.

The urge to go back to myth and primitive art, for instance, had been widespread in Germany before the First World War. The idea of an *Urform* persisted, and can be likened to the first phase of American abstract expressionism when many of the painters sought to uncover the very origins of their inner experiences.

Similarities of experience among individual painters can also be found. Ludwig Kirchner, for instance, while study-ing Rembrandt's sketches, was struck with the idea that he could examine nature, abstract its movements, and create what he called "hieroglyphs." Kirchner's notion of the hieroglyph is in essence equivalent to the American paint-ers' concern with describing the "forces" of nature.

While the Americans claimed the right to paint abstrac-tions that did not depend on nature, they still never con-sented to a painting without "subject." The hieroglyphs of Gottlieb, Guston, Motherwell, Stamos and even Kline, are still extractions from sensible experience.

One other thing the Americans had in common with the earlier German expressionists: their romantic idealism. There was nothing ironic about the young men who formed the Bridge and Blue Rider groups. They were convinced that if they could only purge themselves of their tradition and go down to the intimate source of their passion, they could evolve a "new" painting that would change the course of art.

This enthusiastic missionary fervor found its way to the United States in the person of Hans Hofmann, who is something of a paradox. Although German-born, Hofmann was never a German expressionist. The formative influences in his painting life were predominantly French, but he has an expressionist sensibility par excellence. Hofmann's role in the American movement is difficult to pin down, but there can be no question that in his many years of teaching, he has, in his idiosyncratic way, propagated certain of Kandinsky's basic theorems.

Although Hofmann's philosophy has been flexible, ornamented with timely additions and often remarkably prescient, it remained largely dedicated to the principles of the first decade of the century. He had arrived in Paris in 1904 in time to join the excitement generated by the fauves. He had worked side by side with Matisse in Colorossi's, and he had encountered cubism at its birth.

These three experiences were crucial. Many of his dicta derive directly from them. For instance, when he deplores "tonal" painting and speaks of "pure color" he is amplifying fauve principles. His paintings, with few exceptions, rest on the two pillars of color theory and formal compositional theory.

But he has always been an open spirit, has always listened to strange muses. Clement Greenberg, who followed Hofmann's work for years, credits him with significant premonitions:

The first picture I ever saw in which trickles and spatters of paint became significant form was a Hofmann done in 1943, four years before Pollock found his own way to this technique. Among the first emphatically 'all-over' pictures I ever saw was another Hofmann of around the same date.[2]

If Hofmann was oriented to France in his formal concerns with picturemaking, his temperament — speculative and given to rather garrulous philosophizing — was closer to Germany. And it was through his didactic fervor that certain expressionist principles of Kandinsky, somewhat mitigated by Hofmann's quaint address, filtered through to younger painters from 1936 onward.

Hofmann stressed the "forces" behind the visible, telling his students, "The object should not take importance. There are things bigger to be seen in nature." He urged them to find their symbols (or hieroglyphs), and to "give the most with the least." He repeatedly explained his "cosmology" in which "tensions" in nature must be understood. (His metaphysical, cosmological predilections were fed by a youthful experience in science. As a boy he was adept at mathematics and, among other things, had invented a patented electromagnetic comptometer.)

Hofmann's cosmology was fittingly elastic — one might almost say, fuzzy. But he did emerge with a simple theorem which he felt summed up his message: the idea of Push and Pull. He urged his students to compose so that there was a "synchronized development of both forms and color." He told them that there is an inherent dynamism in plunging line, in brilliant color, in assertive application of paint.

The Push and Pull theory, so simple in its application, bolstered the expressionist urge of his students. In its simplistic form, it served to activate Kandinsky's more profound conception of movement in art. Kandinsky, seeing the significance of movement in painting, envisioned an art of multiple spaces. In his theory, the "center" of a composition was not necessarily visible, and there could be many centers at various stages in space. His own early abstractions were composed of "shapes without apparent connection" occupying different spaces. In a technical analysis of Kandinsky's early abstractions, William Hayter makes it clear:

> In the earliest of Kandinsky's works we see traces of this representation of space, and it is enclosed within the apparent space of the picture. [Referring here to classical perspective.] But after 1915, a different order of space makes an appearance. The basal plane is eliminated and the space figured appears not only to be continuous in all directions, but its co-ordinates are no longer referred to a solid plane. Like interstellar space it is to be referred only to remote points in terms of motion. . . .[3]

The significance of "motion" in painting today is obvious. From Kandinsky's day to the present, the conventional image of a painting as fixed in space has been dormant. Once the "point and line" were activated, it was impossible to imagine a static space.

16 : Music and Painting

THE SEARCH for affinities between music and painting, a favorite pastime of aestheticians even in the days of ancient Greece, took on new meaning as the twentieth century slipped into its hectic course.

Explorers in the nineteenth century had already mapped an itinerary. Throughout the nineteenth century, there were tentative references to "musicality" in painting. The subject was approached confidently by Delacroix, who on several occasions referred to the music of his painting in his journal. "There is a kind of emotion," he wrote, "which is very particularly proper to painting . . . There is an impression which results from an arrangement of colors, light and shadows . . . This is called the music of the picture."

Probably it was from Delacroix that Baudelaire first heard the term "musicality" applied to painting. He in turn referred frequently to what he called the "melodious-ness" of individual pictures, and moved toward an aesthetic which saw the ideal properties of painting in terms of detached rhythmical elements. When he spoke of the "arabesque" in a Delacroix painting, he was alluding to the elements which later in the century became the basis for the symbolist and synthesist movements.

Gauguin, who repeatedly stressed the musical character of his work, and said he considered color as pure vibration just as musical sound is pure vibration, never hesitated to equate his paintings with the work of composers. During the 1880's, it was fashionable to refer to him and his followers as *peintres symphonistes.*

At about the same time, the extreme idealism of Mallarmé began to infiltrate all areas of aesthetic discussion. Mallarmé's insistence on the sovereignty of an inner reality, the "inward arabesque of sound" which shaped his own poems, influenced a whole generation of poets and painters. His vision of the meaning of art is expressed in his essay on the "Crisis in Poetry": "For what is the magic charm of art if not that: that, beyond the book itself, beyond the very text, it delivers up that volatile scattering which we call the Spirit, Who cares for nothing save universal musicality." [1]

Gradually, the concept of universal musicality was altered by developments in philosophy and science. Inevitably time was linked with picture space. The marriage of time and space made by philosophers more than sixty years ago, and consecrated by artists, came to be taken for granted. The nineteenth century had prepared the ground.

Undoubtedly Kandinsky, who more than most painters laid great stress on music, had assimilated *fin de siècle* attitudes when he began his own philosophical research into the relationship of sound to visual symbol. His early writings echo the theoretical statements of the symbolist poets:

"A painter who finds no satisfaction in mere representation, however artistic, in his longing to express his internal life, cannot but envy the ease with which music, the least material of the arts today, achieved this end." As a musical connoisseur, Kandinsky "saw" colors in terms of musical sound, and compositions in terms of musical structures. It was so natural an idiom for him that he related the function of "no color" to the silences in music. He wrote that white is the symbol of a world from which all colors as material attributes have disappeared. This world is too far above us for its "structure" to touch our souls. "There comes a great silence which materially represented is like a cold, indestructible wall going on into the infinite. White therefore, acts upon our psyche as a great, absolute silence like the pauses in music that temporarily break the melody. It is not a dead silence but one pregnant with possibilities. White has the appeal of nothingness that is before birth . . ."[2]

The function of "no color" is well understood by contemporary painters who often leave large areas of their canvases blank, or allow the raw canvas to peer through from beneath. The silences and intervals imagined by Kandinsky have assumed great importance in contemporary painting. In the paintings of Rothko, extensions of a single color sustained like the reverberating chords in a symphony correspond to the long held note in music. Other painters (Kline, de Kooning, Motherwell, for instance) have explored black and white in ways that bear out Kandinsky's "no color" theory; white as symbolizing infinitely extending space, black as movement within that space; or, white as cold silence, black as chromatic intensity. The value of resounding emptiness, known to both Rembrandt and Goya, is heightened in modern abstract painting.

The drift toward a musical understanding of plastic art is reflected in the relationship of avant-garde composers and painters. Not only has the *rapprochement* been felt in the increasing concourse between composers and painters, but it has affected the diction of both music and art criticism. Interchange of terms is found even in journalistic reviewing, as in a 1961 *New York Times* review of a composition by Ralph Shapey, a singularly gifted young avant-garde composer. The writer, Allen Hughes, praises Shapey's free style. "What Mr. Shapey has produced is a composition of abstract expressionism that seems to lay bare the most secret and elemental doubts, yearnings, torments and despairs of the human soul trapped in the chaos of the urban jungle."

The reference to "abstract expressionism" in a music review can only have come about because of the recent contacts between painter and composer. As John Cage has said in his "Lecture on Something," [3] just as formerly "when starting to be abstract, artists referred to musical practises to show that what they were doing was valid, so nowadays, musicians, to explain what they are doing, say 'See, the painters and sculptors have been doing it for quite some time' " (To render this thought I have had to violate Cage's typographical innovations.) Concerts by unorthodox composers such as Cage, Stefan Wolpe, Shapey or Morton Feldman are attended by painters. Paintings are often dedicated to composers, and I know of at least one instance where a painter commissioned a musical composition by a contemporary New York composer.

Whether painters and composers in the avant-garde feel mutual rapport because modern music aspires to the condition of painting and modern painting aspires to the condition of music — the old aesthetic problem which has irritated so many critics — remains unanswerable. Certainly excessive interpretation of one art through another always leads to an impasse. But rather than regard comparisons and parallels as risky, we do better to acknowledge that ultimately, all the arts spring from the same basic sources and kinship is undeniable. A musician's concern with musical space and a painter's concern with plastic rhythm are perfectly consistent.

During the twentieth century since the cubists, music and the visual arts have frequently coincided in their respective theories. The cubists in their experiments with collage incorporated banal everyday materials in the way avant-garde composers introduced everyday sounds such as automobile horns, cannon shots and telephone bells in their compositions. Alfred Barr, in his book on Picasso, describes the collaboration between Jean Cocteau, Erik Satie and Picasso in the ballet "Parade" as follows:

Satie's unassuming music, "like an inspired village band" was to be accompanied by noises, a dynamo, a siren, a telegraph key, an airplane propellor, a typewriter — "ear deceivers" Cocteau called them, employed with the same object as the "eye deceiving" newspapers, facsimile wood grainings and moldings which the cubist painters had used.[4]

The "space-time" concepts of the early avant-garde composers — Satie, Edgard Varèse and George Antheil — were widely discussed by music critics at the time. Relationships between the arts were keenly felt, and even the film was incorporated when the critics spoke of "montages" of sound. Paul Rosenfeld, writing about Varèse and the "it-ness of New York" in his work, said, "Varèse is compelled to give form to his feelings about life, sensations received from the thick current of natural sound in which we dwell." [5] (In the Shapey review quoted above, the writer refers to "the shattering blare of street and machine, the crazy din of the cabaret, the frenzied rush that won't slow down.") Even then, Rosenfeld was able to speak of "some unexplored portion of the cosmos" as the "subject" of Varèse's work. That transcendent note, so familiar in art criticism, was to be sounded again and again in music criticism.

Rosenfeld's description of Varèse's method, in fact, could easily be transposed into the critical terms of the visual arts. He wrote: "Part of Varèse's method involved a number of air-pockets, suspensions of sound between various thematic metamorphoses, and the resulting volumnear accentuation merely augmented the excitement of the emotion."

Varèse himself has felt the kinship between his music and contemporary painting. In 1960, he wrote the text for a catalogue of an abstract painter — unfortunately a dull painter hardly worthy of Varèse's text and the music which

accompanied the exhibition — in which he discussed
form.[6] Form, he said, is the result of process, not a pattern
to be followed. Implying that contemporary painting is involved in the identical process, he went on to describe his
own view of what form is. "I have never tried to fit my
conceptions into a known container." His process he compared to the scientific phenomenon of crystallization:

The crystal is characterized by a definite external form and a
definite internal structure. The internal structure is based on
the unit of crystal which is the smallest group of atoms that
has the order and composition of the substance. The extension
of the unit into space forms the whole crystal. But in spite of
the relatively limited variety of internal structures, the external
forms of crystals are almost limitless . . . Possible musical
forms are as limitless as the exterior forms of crystals.

The concept of the hidden structure that extends itself
in space freely and without preconceived schema (similar
to Mallarmé's concept of the arabesque) is certainly
equally pertinent to painter and composer. The "process"
is unpredictable perhaps, but it is ordered by the artist's
knowledge of the material, and ultimately, as Varèse says,
the work of art "discovers its own form."

Process rather than pattern is basic to the work of
Stefan Wolpe, a composer who has communed with painters since his youth. Life gathers in him and from its re-
serves rushes forth in twitching, vaulting, spinning islands
of sound. In any composition by Wolpe, the voice — a distinct, deeply emotional voice — is heard directly. And
when it ceases, or pauses, the listener sees and hears simultaneously the spaces through which the composer, an in-

finitely susceptible person, has had to navigate. Silences in Wolpe's music correspond closely to Kandinsky's "no color."

In "Forms for Piano, 1959" there are fleeting melismata in a wilderness of changing spaces. But there is "structure." The rushing sounds are "centered" toward the beginning and toward the end by the solid of the plucked note. When Wolpe needs to, he is not afraid to use a conventional chord — a chunk of carved space — to set off the events in the life of the voices. All the vagaries a quick man can know are implicit in Wolpe's music and yet, the ultimate harmony, or form, is always there.

When he is composing for ensemble, as he is in "Enactments for Three Pianos," variation in the three parts contrasts in an almost classical scheme. In the first, the voices rumble up to the surface — the deeper voices in elongated spasms of sound, the upper voice moving out into transparency. The movement of the upper voice, spiraling outward into the thinnest regions, is like the winging line in a painting that flares out from the density of a central form.

In the second enactment the plucked chord is more important. Sounds quicken and shatter like precious wineglasses. A dense patterning of fragile sounds alters the texture. The third opens with a plucked note that resounds and spreads underneath the other struck notes, as the atmosphere that spreads beneath a form in a Guston painting, building slowly, spasmodically, with a mournful knelling. It is sober, taut, melancholy. The repeated plucking is obsessive, like an inner-ear echo or a hallucination. There are attenuated silences, interrupted by a deliberate, em-

phatic scale down, down, steadily down, with muted notes
always knelling. The composition ends on a terse gasp,
perhaps a question.

In Wolpe the islands of sound are dense; they spin, but
not fast enough to lose their materiality. Unlike some of the
younger composers who "do not want to carve out their
musical space," Wolpe does not limit himself to horizontal
composing. He, too, is interested in the problems of the indeterminate, but seems to believe that sound derived from
chance and indeterminacy is only valid when juxtaposed
with the determined.

Morton Feldman, once a student of Wolpe's, has often
devoted himself to a linear, single-dimensional system in
which space, as Frank O'Hara has pointed out, is comparable to the space in certain "all-over" Jackson Pollock paintings.[7] Feldman's direct relationship to the painters has, by
his own admission, influenced his music. "I have always
been interested in *touch* rather than musical forms."

His music — hesitant, reticent, disembodied and non-
symbolic in the sense that the sounds have no reference to
anything but themselves — refuses the architectural tradition of music and aligns itself with the expansive space of
contemporary painting. Still, though his music is supposed
to be totally abstract due to his use of "unpredictability,
chance and spontaneity" in his graphing, or scoring, he
himself describes the effect of one of his pieces "as if you're
not listening but looking at something in nature." By giving the performers great latitude, the composer brings
about a diminution of his own choices, just as a painter
diminishes his choices when he allows a rill of paint to slide

down the canvas's surface unimpeded. Where Wolpe would say that one should mix surprise with enigma, magic and shock, intelligence and abandon, form and anti-form, Feldman would probably take the transcendental attitude that the voice of music — as opposed to noise — is like the first breath of a human, pure and exquisite, uncontaminated by the multiplicity of experience.

John Cage is the most self-consciously transcendental of them all. While painters were obliquely affected by currents from the Orient, and by the buzzing of the "indeterminacy" vogue, Cage studied Oriental philosophies and worked out a system of composition that he said was based on Oriental theories of chance. From the Chinese treatise *I-Ching* he drew inspiration for a compositional system that involved the throwing of dice or coins. In his work, accident, chance, magical metamorphoses and dissociation were carried to an extreme that verges on the absurd. A musical Dadaist in many ways, Cage set out to clean up what he called "inherited aesthetic claptrap."

It is perhaps for this reason that Cage is something of an "artists' artist." He works with materials familiar to the artist but he pushes them so far that they are transformed, often into unmitigated, tedious chaos. Every period in art history has seen someone like Cage who pushes far beyond the norm and sacrifices almost everything, including sensuous continuity, to his obsession. Others benefit by his singleminded audacity. Cage plays a role in music similar to Genet's in literature. Genet is the satanist principle personified, pure and madly consistent: He becomes the cleansing agent by which its opposite is recognized. Through

Genet's diabolic consistency, the morality wanting in his own work is illuminated in the work of others. Similarly, through Cage's addiction to accident, qualities of form and structure are evoked more clearly in others' music.

The significant parallels between Cage's method, which he always calls process, and the method of certain avant-garde painters are implicit in a careful analysis of Cage's working method made by composer Henry Cowell in 1952:[8]

To John Cage, a brief series of sounds, or even a single combination of them has come to seem complete in itself and to constitute an audible "event." . . .

Compare this with statements by abstract expressionist painters who speak of mysteriously emerging "events" in their working process. Also, to the technique of mounting brief series of brush strokes that seem complete in themselves in order to postulate a continuum in space.

But he does not use the conventional organization of music in which such events are related through planned rhythmic, melodic and harmonic successions to produce what we are accustomed to consider an organic musical development.

Similarly, in some abstract expressionist painting there is a strain away from orthodox composition with its laws of balance, symmetry, logical plane recessions and so on. A flare of orange billowing in a corner of a Gorky painting or a great spread of brown sitting heavily on the surface in a Still painting are isolated, autonomous "events" rather than planned into a total harmonic succession of planes as they would be in a traditional cubist painting. The "organic" composition of a Gorky depends on unaccustomed, occult balances.

Instead, since Cage conceives each musical "event" to be an entity in itself that does not require completion, he simply places them one after another and sees them as being related through their co-existence in space, where they are set in a planned order of time. Each event is an aggregate of materials of sound that cohere, making a tiny world of their own, much as the physical elements find themselves joined together in a meteorite. A work of Cage's therefore might easily be likened to a shower of meteors of sound.

The foregoing could be used almost without modification in a discussion of the work of Mark Tobey. Each of the nexuses of line in a Tobey painting becomes an entity in itself that is placed adjacent to another in space. Each of the closely related points in his paintings is actually an "aggregate of materials . . . that cohere, making a tiny world of their own." Cowell's simile of the meteor (one that turns up often in both musical and art criticism) is certainly apt for a description of certain of Tobey's stellar paintings.

Cowell summarizes:

The compositions of Christian Wolff, Morton Feldman, Pierre Boulez and John Cage vary widely in style but a common philosophy unites them: a concentration upon unfamiliar relationships of space and time, and sound and silence, and a conviction that all musical relationships, whether arrived at by chance or by design, have a potential value.

In their experiments with sounds and silences the composers work in the same vein explored by painters who reduced form to atmospheric matrices punctuated by random, floating marks. At the fringes, there are painters who renounce every organizational mode in favor of completely anarchic "marking" in their canvases. Others pick judiciously among the possible relationships. Clyfford Still, for instance, covers huge fields with pitchy blacks in order to leave a lightning bolt of white or yellow and thereby express the "unaccustomed relationships." There are no melodies (line or contiguous planes) and no chords (development in depth) to distract the eye from the spatial expansion.

Pollock wove skeins of line leaving membranous planes between — flutters of silences that never joined in a formal pause but were fluidly shifting. Guston allows a shivering form to intrude in the contained atmosphere that is built like a chord but still subject to the random "event."

The feeling in much contemporary music that there is no beginning and no end but only "aggregate units" corresponds to the feeling in certain abstractions that the heaving rhythms come to no formal conclusion but resume constantly like an ancient bronze dragon with his tail in his mouth. The spaces are circular, baffling, unforeseen.

There are further implications. As long ago as 1920 Erik Satie ironically proposed his *musique d' ameublement*, explaining that "furniture music creates vibration; it has no other goal; it fills the same role as light and heat." Although Satie was undoubtedly half-serious, the idea of enveloping sound has persisted. Its counterpart in painting is "environmental painting," the name given, I think, by Clement Greenberg to the huge canvases that came in the wake of Jackson Pollock and which are intended to absorb the spectator, to enclose him in an environment rather than force him into a frontal relationship to their surface. Barnett Newman, whose gigantic paintings of a single hue, divided by a single thin line, are specifically intended to work as invisibly as light or heat on the spectator's sensibilities, typifies the tendency. They are "background" paintings which make themselves felt as presences rather than objects.

Again, we are back in the presence of romanticism, and of the longing for infinity. Even in musical terminology, the word "infinite" has been reiterated constantly since the mid-nineteenth century when critics spoke of the "infinite melody" of Wagner. The diction of music criticism, like that of art criticism, has pretty consistently held the romantic note.

An article on avant-garde music by André Boucourechliev, a French critic, stresses the clean break with the past beginning with Schoenberg, and culminating in what he calls the most hermetic phase in Western music: the strict application of the serial principle.[9] "It is at this moment of musical absolutism — between 1952 and 1955 — that electronic music is born. It appears then as the instrument par excellence for taking integral possession of the universe of sound in its continuity."

Boucourechliev's diction becomes increasingly abstract as he continues his outline. Musical language, he says, liberated from all pre-existing conditions, leaps all laws other than that, always renewed, which rediscovers itself constantly. "For the univocal trajectory of the work of the past, with its ineluctable termination, predictable and reassuring, is substituted now the aleatory — a musical time open to a thousand possibilities." Serial music, he continues, has become a "form of thought, a manner of living time in its discontinuity and its absence of finality . . . That which the composer composes is now the *probable* visage of his work, a network of possibilities rather than forms fixed once and for all."

Openness — the need this critic feels for the vault into unbounded spaces, and his unrestrained diction to match those spaces — is typical of both music and art criticism after the Second World War. The emphasis on spaces that are not codified, not contained within any system, occurs in both avant-garde music and painting. Space and time commingled have opened both arts to a plethora of possibilities — and possibly, to many impossibilities.

17 : Space: The House We Inhabit

P ROBABLY SPACE as an isolated element was never so widely discussed in the arts before. Or, for that matter, in the sciences. In a book on the evolution of scientific thought, A. D'Abro sketches the new dimensions physics had liberated at the turn of the century, raising questions that have since preoccupied speculative minds:

"The essence of Riemann's discoveries consists in having shown that there exist a vast number of possible types of spaces, all of them perfectly consistent. When, therefore, it comes to deciding which of these possible spaces real space will turn out to be, we cannot prejudge the question." [1]

To the painter all conceived spaces have a reality. It is not a question of judging at all but only one of experiencing and articulating. Since 1900, painters have been able to compound unlimited fantasies of space. Moholy-Nagy, when he wrote *The New Vision,* was able to list no less than forty-five kinds of space available to the artist, among them crystalline, cubic, hyperbolic, metric, fictive, limitless, *n*-dimensional, elliptical and so on.

Fantasies of space floriating in recent art theory are often the source of confusion. It becomes increasingly difficult to understand the words "time-space" as they flit through the texts of artists and art critics. Some of the younger contemporary painters have fallen prey to space-time jargon, imagining "space" only in its superficial sense — literally superficial. To them, unbounded space, or space-time, represents a surface spread. If they paint a canvas large enough, and if they spread forms on the surface to a point that they seem to go beyond the four boundaries, they are satisfied that they have achieved an expansive expression of space-time.

The elaboration of space fantasies in American painting has its specific background. It has often been noticed — and I'm inclined to believe justifiably — that the American affection for what is both literally and figuratively vast can be interpreted on a simple geographical basis. Americans have long been wilderness painters, impressed by America's continental breadth. Even the nineteenth-century painter Winslow Homer resorted to almost abstract means to get the vastness across. When he painted the endless flanks of the mountains crowding the sky, he deliberately exaggerated the horizontal axis. Sometimes, in fact, the horizon disappears entirely in his paintings. The reality of the open spaces he knew intimately was so compelling that, ultimately, only an abstract metaphor could cover the experience.

In the purely environmental sense, it is understandable that Europeans rarely have felt the need to align themselves with vast nature. Their transcendental paintings remain within a normal format usually since they don't have the continental vision behind them reminding them of overwhelming physical reality. It is partly for this reason that European abstract artists are not troubled with the ideas of "content" and "subject" as Americans are. Their flights into the nonmaterial world, or cosmos-at-large, or time-space, are purely imaginary, removed from the virtual fact of vastness.

In order to understand the image of space in modern painting, it is not enough to speak of "expanding" space or space continua. There must be a search for the very sources of the spatializing imagination. At the level of origins, space and time are always mingled.

It is easier to discuss origins in terms of poetry. The poet's imagining mind is able to shift far back in time and space to locate for us symbols deeply embedded in human history. When St.-John Perse writes of the sea he tells us of an immensity that resides in us, stirs us immediately for reasons that are not easily put to the word. We know the sea, or desert, or sky, in our own depths without the aid of an oceanographer's handbook or a chemical analysis of salt. In this way we recognize the swoop of a line in a de Kooning painting as an evocation of his experience of sea, landscape and a multitude of other imaginative experiences.

The spaces Perse imagines, traversed by natural and human events, are containers of time: time that perhaps exists independently only within the imagining mind. He "places" us first, then weaves us to and fro, shuttling through vast times and spaces. Perse operates in what Marcel Raymond has called "the great free spaces of the modern fantastic" — those reverberating spaces that have always haunted poets and painters but have found special emphasis in the nineteenth and twentieth centuries.

Parallels in the vision of painters and poets are unavoidable in this context. The intimacy of poets and painters in France since the nineteenth century and their mutual influence must not be overlooked. Furthermore, the modern tradition acquired by Americans from recent history was based on prior developments in France. The currents of pictorial and literary expression in late nineteenth-century France flow together too often to be entirely gratuitous. Certainly Mallarmé's friendship with the avant-garde painters of his day nourished, or at least confirmed, his own aesthetic theory. His touching tributes to Redon, Manet, Gauguin and other painters who attended his Tuesday evenings are scattered throughout his correspondence.

Mallarmé recognized that space in conventional language was "a surface traversed by a uniform and irreversible movement," according to Maurice Blanchot.[2] "To this space Mallarmé restores depth. A phrase doesn't content itself with rolling on in a linear manner, it opens itself." In Mallarmé's space, instants do not succeed each other in horizontal sequence but are compounded on several levels.

Even in the earlier poems, such as the celebrated "Brise Marine," Mallarmé's spaces spread and overlap in complex sequences that easily suggest comparisons with modern painting. He takes us from the idea of "fleeing beyond" to the unlimited spaces of sea and sky. Then suddenly he is back to "the old gardens reflected by your eyes." Then he veers to a great abstraction, the night, only to particularize his experience of the night by mentioning "the barren light of my lamp/On the blank paper whose whiteness forbids," giving us the confined space of his chamber. Throughout this poem, Mallarmé skids vertiginously in time and space. The imagery wells out in thousands of collateral allusions. The space in contemporary painting refers as much to the "depth" of experience as sensed by Mallarmé as it does to its surface extension.

A few writers have attempted to study the spatializing imagination in scientific terms but they rarely confront the experiences we know intimately and that are beyond the reach of descriptive language. Perse's or Mallarmé's experience of the sea, or de Kooning's experience of landscape, are available to us only in the language of images.

A French philosopher, Gaston Bachelard, is one of the few writers who has had the courage to undertake the task of sorting out the language of images and the functions of the imagining mind without drowning in a morass of abstractions. Bachelard applies an original, deliberately non-scientific method.[3] He explains in *The Poetics of Space* that after working nearly a lifetime observing the disciplines of scientific method, he discovered that they were hindrances rather than aids when at last he came to study the creative imagination. His conscious attempt to free himself from the scientific laws of causality resulted in this brilliant study of space, in which he eschews all the methods of the sciences, even psychoanalysis, which, he says, "explains the flower by its fertilizer." He is interested only in what he calls "the lived space" and not the space of the geometer.

The "lived" space, he says, far from being a circumscribed chamber or a geometer's cube, is a dynamic, constantly shifting product of the imagination. He speaks of the primary shelter to illustrate his thesis: The primary shelter is a nongeometric space, the house of man. "Our soul is a dwelling," he declares. "It is because the memories of former dwellings are relived as reveries that the dwellings of the past are imperishable in us." Explaining further: "We think sometimes we know ourselves in time but what we know is only a suite of fixations in the spaces of the stability of the being, being which doesn't want to flow, which even in the past . . . wants to suspend the flight of time. In its thousands of cells, space holds time compressed."

The image of a man's house, and of houses or shelters in general, serves Bachelard as an incredibly flexible analogue of human existence. A man's house is more than an object, he insists. It is a cosmos — our first universe and one to which we keep referring throughout our waking and dreaming lives:

The childhood house is physically inscribed in us. It is a group of organic habits. After twenty years and in spite of all the anonymous staircases, we will find again the reflexes of the first staircase. The childhood house has inscribed in us the hierarchy of the diverse functions of inhabiting. We are the diagram of the functions of inhabiting that house, and all other houses are only variations on the fundamental theme. . . . In this dynamic community of man and house, in this dynamic rivalry of house and universe, we are far from any reference to simple geometric forms. The house lived in is not an inert box. . . ."

In this dynamic house of Bachelard's, in which windows, cellars, attics, stairs and intimate corners each have specific qualities when evoked by the imaginations of poets, there can be no such thing as a static image of an event in time or in space. Everything in the imagination works on everything else. This house, metaphorically speaking, is the house of the contemporary painter, for in his work, no single form is intended to be independent or measurable in the geometric sense. When Philip Guston paints what appears to be a scale with its two teetering weights, he does not paint it as an object set in a defined space, as would a Renaissance painter. He makes it instead "a diagram of the function of inhabiting"; a sign which partakes of all the whispering forms in the background and all the ambiguous currents coursing over the foreground.

Lived space, or the space that is compounded in the imagination, is so flexible that it can shift into abstractions that are not directly dependent on objects. Space, Bachelard says, is immanent in our reveries, in the solitudes that bring forth works of art:

Here [in solitude] space is everything because time no longer animates memory. Memory — strange that it is — doesn't register concrete duration in the Bergson sense. One cannot relive abolished durations. It is through space, it is in

space that we find the beautiful fossils of concrete duration
. . . To locate a memory in time can only matter to a biog-
rapher . . . More urgent than the determination of dates for
the understanding of intimate space is the localization in the
spaces of our interior.

For Bachelard the image strikes deep and has a thousand
reverberations. It touches the depths before it moves the
surface, as he says. "The poetic image is not an echo of
the past. It is more the reverse: by the brilliance of an image the distant past resounds with echoes." The suddenness
of an image's apparition, and his conviction that no "culture" really prepares us for its uniqueness, leads Bachelard
to believe that no amount of archeological, epistemologi-
cal or psychological research can "explain" an image.

Similarly, no amount of iconographical or stylistic research wholly "explains" an image in painting. Artists
have often spoken of the strangeness of certain of their images. They have remarked that their own paintings at first
seemed to come from unknown sources and that only after
the first flash of recognition were they able to "associate"
the forms. Such images are equivalent to the poetic images
that Bachelard says touch the depths before they touch the
surface. They communicate first with out own spatializing
imagination.

How imagery expands in the imagination is very well
demonstrated by Bachelard's own expansion from the first
idea of shelter. One aspect of shelter, he points out, is
refuge. "The person who experiences the sentiment of
refuge locks himself within himself, retires, is absorbed
. . . All the verbs which describe the dynamics of retreat

reflect animal movements, movements of coiling in . . ." These movements, associated in his mind with shells and nests, are characterized as primary images: images which solicit in the reader or viewer a sense of primitivity, of withdrawing into a corner. The sense of entanglement and of being "in" the picture which obsessed Jackson Pollock might easily be seen in Bachelard's terms of primary image. Everyone knows the experience of retreating inward, be it into a corner, a cozy lamplit room, a thicket of trees, or underneath the covers of one's bed.

Such a primary image of "protection" as the nest also inspires Bachelard with a host of reveries, demonstrating the resounding character of images. Once one loves an image, he says, it cannot any more be a copy of a fact. To prove his point he cites Jules Michelet, writing on the architecture of birds. The bird, says Michelet, is a worker deprived of tools. The tool is the body of the bird itself, its breast with which it presses and squeezes the material until it renders them absolutely viable. Within the nest, the instrument which imposes a circular form on the nest is nothing other than the body of the bird. The house then is the person itself, taking its form and its most immediate effort. "The result," writes Michelet, "is only obtained by constantly repeated pressure of the chest. Not one of these blades of grass which, in order to take and keep the curve, has not been a thousand times pushed by the breast, the heart, certainly with labored breathing, with palpitation . . ." Thus, says Bachelard, values displace facts.

The space within the nest so vividly "lived" in Michelet's imagination is clearly a humanized space, one which the

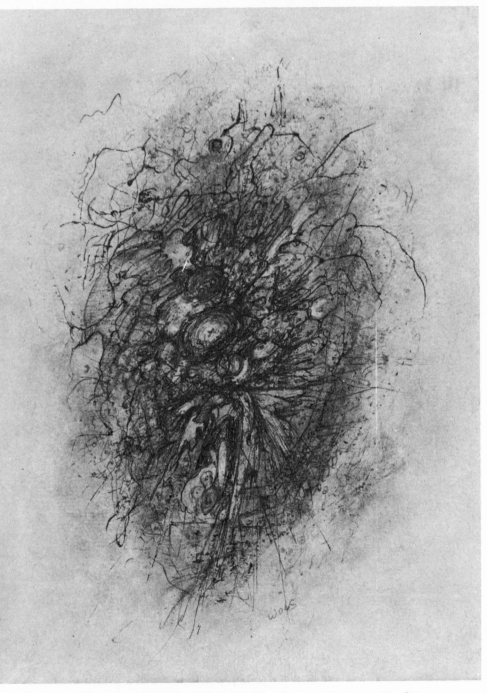

WOLS (Alfred Otto Wolfgang Schulze), *The Nests,* 1948. Aquarelle, 6⅔ x 5.

(Cordier-Warren Gallery, New York)

author probably never rationalized. He "loved" the image and let it speak directly. Such loved images are frequent in the visual arts. Most of the watercolors Wols painted in the middle to late 1940's offer again and again an image of involuted, curving lines that have a distinct nestlike form. All the wiry, microscopic lines lead inward, to a spherical void. These images take their shape not only from the energy concentrated in the central portion of Wols's composition, but from the atmosphere that always seems to echo the insistently curving shapes within, pushing them and pressing them into the integral cosmos-in-little that was Wols's dream.

The space that Wols presents is not "factual" but the product of a spatializing imagination. If we were to apply Bachelard's method (a phenomenological method that examines only the given) to Wols's paintings, we would have to ask *not* Where does it come from, but rather, *what* is it? Through absolute attention to and total absorption in a work of art, Bachelard derives an irreducible image — an image which instantly moves him and depends little on cultural background.

One of the best irreducible images Bachelard cites is a line from the French writer Henri Bosco: *"Un long arbre frémissant touche toujours l'âme."* (The trembling of a tall tree always touches the soul.) Here there is no "objective" basis for analysis any more than there would be if we tried to give an objective explanation of Van Gogh's cypress trees quivering in the wind. Enough souls have been moved, as Bachelard demonstrates in a large group of quotations concerning trees responding to the wind, to make it apparent that this is an irreducible image.

The very word "soul" defies analysis and has all but dropped out of the modern poet's vocabulary. A contemporary American poet to whom I showed Bosco's line commented that the modern English-writing poet would have written: The Selfhood is touched by the trembling of a tall tree. But Bachelard, who accepts that which is given, retains the concept of the soul. It exists in language and that is enough. A tree and its trembling is not a transitive metaphor. It is an image that penetrates our imagination so deeply that its antecedents are irrelevant.

Transposing Bachelard's method to painting, I could say that if we concentrate our attention on what is "given" in one of Monet's lily-pond canvases, we would have to challenge many interpretations of Monet's vision. Cézanne was supposed to have said that Monet was "only an eye." Historians often point out that Monet himself insisted he wanted only to record what he saw with the greatest possible accuracy. Such observations have led interpreters to exclude discussion of Monet's tendency to abstraction. These interpreters commit the sin of intentional fallacy. They avert their minds from the imponderabilia that form the core of a work of art. Whatever Monet may have said — and painters are not given to accurate exegeses of the meaning of their work — we must strive to see in the work what Bachelard would call its "resonance," its imaginative breadth and not its literal limitation.

What Monet had, and what all great artists have, was the gift of profound attention. At a certain point, attention to detail becomes hallucinating, and it is here that art begins. Genius leaps forward, leaving behind the chaos and disparateness of what the eye perceives reaching for the radiance of a totality. If we describe Monet's quest as a quest for optical accuracy, as is so often done, then the true image is obscured. No matter how deeply concerned Monet was with transcribing what he saw, he went finally beyond what he saw and knew into a realm that Poe would have called supernal.

Monet was a poet of water. His seas, even as a youth when he still separated forms with sparkling, clear atmosphere, were reflections of his skies and vice versa. The slender strand between these great containers of human imagination was often swept away in the magnitude of his concentration. Monet had inherited from his time the idea that he must fix appearances. But the struggle was uncongenial to his temperament. Monet knew that the fluid elements of light on water and sky would release him from the mundane bounds of his own convictions and those of his Impressionist colleagues, and permit him to go beyond.

In the "Lily Pond" series, as he went deeper and deeper into his subject, or rather, as his attention intensified, his strokes became abstractions of water and surrounding foliage. They enabled him to express the envelope, the unifying principle he had been seeking for more than forty years. The long calligraphic stroke, so accented in these paintings and in his pictures of wisteria blooms, came to be more than a writing impulse — it was Monet's means of transcending his own previous rules. With it he could forget about the proper distance for "seeing" his painting; he could enclose his circular universe with its curve. The surfaces of the "Lily Pond" paintings became abstractions in the highest sense. His imagination moved ahead of his

CLAUDE MONET, *The Japanese Footbridge*, 1920-1922. Oil, 35¼ x 45⅞.

(The Museum of Modern Art, New York)

brush, intermingled sky, water and movement, erased conventional boundaries between surfaces, saw inner currents and corresponding outer forms that the "objective" eye would never see. Furthermore, no objective experience could prepare us for Monet's image. Only the musing imagination that has traveled in these imaginary spaces could grasp his image in its irreducible potency.

Bachelard's idea that inhabited or lived space transcends geometrically measured space provides a way to think about paintings in which structure is not immediately apparent. Just as in the imagination nothing is static, in contemporary painting there is a tendency to avoid stasis, particularly the static notion of traditional perspective. The spaces many painters imagine today are in the process of constant transformation. They are not copies of observed facts but amalgams of experienced spaces. Even the outwardly tranquil canvases of Mark Rothko are far removed from the geometer's measured space. Although Rothko uses quadrilateral shapes, they hover and tremble in their assigned spaces and, on long perusal, seem to stir in a dreamlike way, much as our imaginations move in reverie.

A certain obsessiveness inheres in the metamorphosing spaces our painters reveal. It occurs in much the same way that certain words are repeated by Baudelaire. These repeated words, according to Bachelard, brought Baudelaire into the realm of the imagination that is independent of observable facts. For example, Baudelaire used the word "vast" incessantly, often incongruously. "Vast" is a serene word, a vocable of breathing, "a grave word, enemy of turbulence. It is necessary that the word 'vast' reign over the

peaceful silence of the being." The word itself became
talismanic, transporting Baudelaire into a willed abstract
space in which his imagination was set free.

The repetition of an image lived in painting should be
considered talismanic too. Just as Baudelaire was able to
keep his imagery fresh by surrounding the incantatory word
"vast" with vivid concrete symbols, so the painter is able
to give fresh form each time to the fundamental lived image. Obsessiveness, such as Wols's and Pollock's insistence
on closure; Guston's leaving a breathing space of white
canvas almost invariably; Brooks's swirling great curving
strokes that plummet like waterfalls, is a reflection of a
unique way of living in space and should be read as such.

The "lived" space in painting is recognized swiftly. The
most simple apprehension of depth, falling, closure, openness is its response. When, in a Tworkov painting, the nar-
row interstice between the foreplane and the shadowy
drama behind it is seized by the imagination, it is seized immediately. When, in a de Kooning, there is a dip into
space, a tunnel into depth, the imagination quickly assim-
ilates it and might, if it were Bachelard's imagination, re-
late it to sensations of shelter, of the cave, of the attic —
sensations that can be both pleasant and unpleasant, stifling
and cozy.

These irreducible images, corresponding to the most
simple basic emotions, are at the heart of the visual experience. Once seized in their immediacy, both the sense and
the mind can "work" the image, filling out the experience.

18 : Science, Art and Intuition

In RECENT YEARS many scientists have paid homage to artists' insights. They have come to recognize affinities between their own working procedures and those of the artist. Einstein often said that he believed intuition and inspiration were essential to scientific thought since "knowledge is limited, whereas imagination embraces the entire world."

Scientists who have remarked similarities between modern science and art begin with a simple observation: The twentieth-century scientist differs from scientists of the past in that he now knows that he is a part of the thing he studies. This discovery — that the observer is a significant part of the thing observed — has radically altered his attitude. Artists have demonstrated that they, too, realized that they were a significant part of the thing observed. As soon as this happened, as it did with Cézanne, who almost certainly was unfamiliar with scientific news in his day, the course of painting was affected. These discoveries coincided in history.

Such coincidences in the separate realms of science and art can be enumerated at length. Lancelot Law Whyte, a leading scientist who has followed developments in the arts thoughtfully, has even credited the artist with prevision.[1] "It is interesting to note," he said in a public lecture, "that the intuitive mind of the artist may have anticipated a development in exact science. For the dissonances and tensions of painting and music of recent decades surely express the élan of asymmetry, the imperfections, differences and tensions which initiate the movement toward a more perfect and stable form. The classical idea of static perfection or harmony is being complemented by a deeper recognition of the real disharmonies which provoke change and growth."

The anticipating intuitive mind of the artist, his prevision, has proved itself many times over in the history of art. Anticipation occurred not only in special instances, such as Leonardo, equally gifted in science and art, but in the cases of artists whose interests were circumscribed and whose only passion was to paint. The imagination, "embracing the entire world," could postulate fantasies that became facts in the course of scientific history.

Ruysdael, living in the seventeenth century, knew nothing of airplanes though the legend of flying as epitomized by Icarus was known to him as it had been to Breughel the Elder. Flying resides deep in man's psyche and its representation in the visual arts has a continuous history. Not only was Ruysdael ignorant of the way the world looks to the flying traveler, he was also ignorant of the way landscape looks from great heights, living as he did in Holland, a country of flatlands.

Yet in certain of his paintings, Ruysdael imagined himself in mid-air. In those deep landscapes where the earth seems to slide back into infinity and the clouds sweep up in a great expansive mass, Ruysdael painted as if he were suspended. (He was not the only or the first painter in history to do this, but he offers as good an example as any.) The sky and flatlands then become like a giant open clam joined at the horizon and embracing — midway between its yawning shells — visionary man. Sky is more than a canopy, earth more than a horizontal floor. They merge in a transcending vision that is greater than the facts Ruysdael set out to record.

Even old-master artists did not often paint what they *knew* of the world, but what they could imagine about it. At the full development of his genius, many an old-master painter has intimated the way future generations would see the universe, and even, as Whyte points out, presaged developments in scientific observation. Titian was more than eighty when he painted "The Rape of Europa." He was thoroughly versed in Renaissance principles of perspective and could very well have used its conventions if he chose. Europa could have been painted sitting firmly on the bull instead of being queerly suspended in a foreground space.

But Titian was no longer interested in objectively

TITIAN, *The Rape of Europe*, 1562. Oil, 70$\frac{1}{10}$ x 80$\frac{1}{5}$.

(Courtesy of The Isabella Stewart Gardner Museum, Boston)

known spaces. He defied all the rules. The water sinks far below eye level while Europa soars upward. The soft sky both recedes and comes forward in one of the most ambiguous and complex visions ever painted before the late nineteenth century. Titian established a host of unorthodox relationships which suggested flux and the merging of elements. The dialectic between large and small, near and distant, is not the clear symmetrical relationship usual in his time. On the contrary, it approaches the fantastic spaces familiar in modern poetry and painting. And, with its accent on ambiguity, it suggests the climate of thinking in current sciences.

"For so long science seemed to be setting up a triumph of reason," poet Stanley Kunitz has observed, "but now it is restoring mystery to the universe. In our time we do not have a steady gaze on a fixed reality. The view of our universe is one of statistics and probabilities without cause and effect."

At one time it was possible to use the word "atom" in its original sense: a substance that is indivisible, a unity that cannot be reduced. But now, though we still use the word, its meaning has disconcertingly slipped away. Atoms are now considered microcosms with very complicated systems within systems, many of which have yet to be understood. Electrons, protons, neutrons and now mesons are all particles beyond the atom. There is no ultimate indivisible unity known to us at this time. Everything that scientists report seems to point to a total dissolution of matter as we know it, posing a depressing problem.

If indeed the artist or scientist is a part of the thing observed, how does he isolate himself from this ultimate de-materialization? How does he preserve his faith in an entity, in himself? Even what Kunitz calls the "moral universe" in which the artist maintains "probity of self" is subject to being part of the thing observed.

The implications of these problems have not escaped scientists. Poincaré asked if the laws of nature, when considered as existing outside of the mind that creates or observes them, are intrinsically invariable. He answered that the question was insoluble. The disturbing aspect of discoveries that seem to defy all previous laws is implicitly expressed by D'Abro when he says:[2]

The physicist and the mathematical physicist are compelled to operate and reason *as though they believed* in the real existence of a real absolute objective universe, one of space and time, according to classical science; one of space-time, according to the theory of relativity. In fact, as we have said, were it impossible to conceive of a common objective world, one existing independently of the observer . . . physical science would be impossible. [Italics mine.]

This impossibility exists, at least in creative minds. The unpredictability of phenomena being demonstrated now by scientific experiment has long been known to artists. One could say that it is the "subject" of many works of art even before the nineteenth century. The artist knows that mystery is a constant in human existence. This is a fact that scientists and intellectuals often find difficult to confront.

The "good sense" which underlies all previous materialistic philosophies is demonstrably undermined. Bergier and

Pauwels give the following example.[3] In physics, they say, a proposition can now be both true and false. The same entity can now be both continuous and discontinuous. They describe an experiment:

Take a piece of paper. Make two holes close to one another. It is evident to common sense that an object small enough, in order to pass through these holes, will pass either through one or the other. In the eyes of common sense an electron is an object. It possesses a definite weight, it produces a luminous light when it strikes the television screen, a shock when it hits the microphone. There is our object small enough to pass through one of our two holes. Now, observation with an electronic microscope shows us that the electron passes at the same time through both holes . . . It's crazy, but it's experimental. . . . it is the very structure of our reason that we must modify in order to understand . . .

If scientists are concerned with new relationships, the mysteries, dissonances and disharmonies within nature, and if, like the authors quoted above, they can no longer believe in the symmetrical logic of thesis and antithesis, they come very close to the artist's position. They share with the artist a need to establish order in their observations and, like the artist, they recognize that an established order must sooner or later give way to a new, entirely different order.

Sometimes an "avant-garde" scientific theory stimulates a creative mind to leap into a zone that brings him close to the origin of contemporary art. Sometimes the leap has already been made and scientific theory merely confirms it. When Julien Alvard, a critic whose writing is so original that he becomes an artist, forced his thought into the twen-

tieth century — which is to say beyond Freud and the ma‐
terialists' laws of causality — he found a scientist whose theory seemed to confirm his own intuitions, which were in turn confirmed by works of contemporary art.

Alvard's discovery of Stéphane Lupasco's 1951 essay "The Principle of Antagonism and the Logic of Energy" altered his perception and inspired him to vault into the regions charted by painters. Alvard grasped Lupasco with his imagination.[4] "Lupasco's idea, based chiefly on the de‐ velopment of microphysics, opened a field far wider than the customary concept of the organization of the universe," he wrote. "Here was a confrontation of two processes of logic, the one reasoning in terms of similarities, the other in terms of singularities." Lupasco's theory of diversifica‐ tion, according to Alvard, "provided a means of reinte‐ grating into terrestrial development — not as an exception but as a rule — phenomena regarded as heterogeneous, confused, indeterminate, untimely or merely novel." A "third matter" designated by Lupasco, and too complicated to attempt to describe here, embrace both similarities and singularities, "and maintained them in antagonistic equilib‐ rium."

All three of Lupasco's "matters" are nothing other than energy. As he says, the notion of an element must be re‐ placed by the notion of an event. The only way "matter" in its conventional sense occurs is through oppositions, con‐ flicts and antagonisms existent in energy. Without those contradictory and often inexplicable forces, we would have only homogeneity, or inertness, which is equivalent to death. Heterogeneity and diversity are life itself, occuring only by virtue of the dynamic antagonisms inherent in energy.[5]

Excited by Lupasco's unorthodox propositions, Alvard "saw" paintings in their terms. The calligraphic rhythms of Tobey, the improvisations of Mathieu, the gestures of Kline and Pollock, appeared to him as expressions of energy actualized by contradictory, unseen forces. The tachiste painters with their asymmetrical compositions, their wandering amorphous forms and diffuse colors, seemed to illustrate Lupasco's teeming universe of energy without a fixed center.

Admitting these seemingly endless contradictions and unclassified antagonisms, Alvard's mind continued to search for possible links in a chain of ultimate unity. His search for equilibrium, even antagonistic equilibrium, is no different from that of the artist who, no matter how disparate his materials, hopes to know the boundaries of his cosmos. The most occult of modern painters strives to attain a philosophical basis for his work which is the same as giving order or form to his observations.

As it is art and not classifiable nature that the imagining mind is dealing with, the search for order is pursued without hope of proof. The creative mind must live with assumptions and riddles. The paradox is that the artist — even the abstract informal artist — does make use of logic, but he uses it to reach a supralogical level of feeling.

A dramatic illustration is Paul Valéry's application of logic in order to arrive ultimately at the supralogical. In *L'Idée Fixe* Valéry uses the dialogue to explore space and form from every possible point of attention.[6] Nothing lasts in the spirit, he says, everything there is transitive. The sequence of psychic life, if one registers it, would show a perfect disorder, a discontinuity that the irregularity of a fly's flight represents perfectly.

Yet, having stated the maze of irregularities, Valéry in this dialogue strains to discover an ideal order. He speaks of the universe as a "gigantic work," working toward supreme thought. Matter loses itself, he tells us, but form lives on:

— Concede that there is a mental work which tends to form, or to construct . . . or rather, to let a thing form, a system of which a part or certain conditions are given . . . in any case, I am sure of one thing: nothing is more rare than the faculty of co-ordinating, harmonizing, orchestrating a large number of parts.

Yet, difficult as it is, Valéry persists in trying to discover the essence of that "mental work which tends to form." He suggests that it strives to envision the Unity of Nature:

— Observe that it is a question of nothing less than pursuing and defining the Unity of Nature.
— But what proves to me that there *is* a unity in nature?
— That is exactly the question I posed to Einstein. He answered me: *It is an act of faith.*

To make original thinking possible, Valéry is suggesting, it is necessary to make that act of faith. The *idée fixe* itself, transformed many times in the course of the dialogue, is endowed with an excitability that makes everything else seem small. Valéry invents the word "omnivalent" to cover this idea. The omnivalent idea "hooks onto everything and is hooked by everything."

Alvard too touches on this notion of contingency: "Art, still and forever in search of truth, is at grips with manifold and subjective impressions and struggles to depict these, not by defining them, but by interweaving in one sentence or on one page all that gravitates towards them at a given moment."

Even the idea that hooks onto everything and is hooked by everything, as do the images in many contemporary paintings, ultimately has a purpose. Although fragmentation and dissociation are characteristics of modern art, they act in search of ultimate equilibrium.

Among serious artists today the purpose is, as it always was, to discover and define the spaces in which human life transpires. They are only too ready to perform the act of faith Einstein prescribed.

19 : Artist on the Unknown · Shore

WHEN WE FIND repeated references to "cosmic" painters, composers and writers, we are forced to confront the equivocal concept known as the cosmos. In dictionary definition, a cosmos is "the universe conceived as an orderly, harmonious system; any self-inclusive system characterized by order and harmony."

All random activity in the arts, all fragmentations and echoes of myths, all demands for liberation, ultimately serve to test the existence of a "self-inclusive system" which is the artist himself. If the contemporary artist denies systems, he does not deny himself.

It may seem difficult to discern the search for a self-inclusive system in the work of a Dadaist, or a linear composer, or a writer like Kerouac who denies editorial imposition of form on his writing. But then, our century has seen many paradoxes. We have seen artists turn outward to the skies or seas or outer-space in order to find inner meanings. We have seen explorations of different spaces — the spaces of militarists, of scientists, of artists. We have seen man rushing into authentic extraterrestrial situations, orbiting the earth and raking the floors of the seas. A passionate skin-diver was asked to explain his perilous hobby and replied, "We're looking for something — God knows what it is. It's not adventure and thrills. There are certain words that come close to describing it — mystery, intrigue, beauty, silence, freedom . . ."

The skin-diver doesn't "know" what he is looking for. Yet he thinks of words, albeit abstract words, to describe conditions that are "self-inclusive." Silence is enormous, full, an entity. The artist, the skin-diver, the aviator (St. Exupéry), the geophysicist and the microphysicist are looking.

There are dangers. There are always dangers in commitments to the unknown. There is the danger that in the vagueness of the abstract dialogue with the universe, concrete experience will be submerged, smothered in dead language as are certain political philosophies. In their flight into the spaces of their imaginations many artists have diminished their choices willfully and are left with only their "sign" and no cosmos at all. Many have ceded to the very forces they are fighting. Although mass communication is the enemy, the artist is tempted to use the techniques — repetition and hawking — to assert his difference. Sometimes he mistakes his sign or chant for his cosmos.

The largest part of twentieth-century writing and painting, as we have seen, has been deliberately experimental. The desire to explore the obscure margins of human experience has been far greater than the desire to impose individual order on known experiences. This is the still vital legacy of nineteenth-century romanticism.

The transcendentalism that marks so much of our art has been abetted by history. Flights to the moon affect the artist and the community within which the artist operates. The existence of demonic end-of-the-world possibilities, so different from the apocalyptic crises of the past, has penetrated the consciousness of men at all levels of culture. The fact that life can be extinguished from one moment to the next is acknowledged. As a result, man affronts an absolute situation. The possibility of disaster is known to be dependent on events. Disaster will be the result of man-made history. It is not as if some angry god hammers the world to bits. It is worse, for the gods usually repent and re-create, but man knows himself capable of total, unregenerate destruction.

The artist — the man of conscience, or at least of acute consciousness — exists in a situation that the most ordinary of men know to be absolute and he gives his response: He turns away from the world as it anxiously ticks off its moments of grace and seeks to find a means out of the snare of history. He responds to an absolute situation with an absolute image. There are many examples: Clyfford Still paints the suffocating surface of life — or is it the abyss? — and, with a small-toothed saw, carves out a little eternal breathing place for himself. Mark Rothko finds a beginning, remembering for us the moments when all was well with the world, and also the dark stirrings of disaster. But these images are far away, well removed from the individual events of life here and now.

In a sense the artist has removed himself from the community. When, after the Second World War, the artist spoke, he spoke against the community, insisted his language was cryptic, and proudly declared his right to seem unintelligible in view of the risks he was taking.

But risks for whom? Not only for himself since the artist remains at heart a man of faith who believes that what he has to express about himself can be generalized for all humanity. Polemically the artist walked out on society. In reality he became more necessary than ever.

As we have seen, one of the first thoughts occurring to the American avant-garde was the reinstatement of a subject in painting. By "subject" they didn't mean a narrative subject or even observed facts. They meant a subject that resided deep in the human psyche, that could outlive and outwit time and events. In turning to myth, Pollock, Rothko, Still, sought to find the moment of life that was at the beginning and that has been relived generation by generation regardless of historical events. It happened with the writers, as well, who were weary with empiricism and exhumed Oedipus, Ulysses, Sisyphus and Daedalus because their stories have resisted all movements and styles and remained models of human existence. In other words, while historical events stirred anxiety each day, the artist moved out of their range.

Or at least he tried to. He tried to prepare himself to

withstand the shocks that the demonic had in store for him in order that his will to create would survive. The Second World War was only the beginning of a series of throttling shocks. It put an end to the dreamed possibility of social justice (artists in the 1930's were genuinely preoccupied with such problems) and opened an epoch of enormities no man of conscience could accept.

A good example of the crumbling hopes in the 1940's was the avant-garde magazine *Dyn*, published in Mexico in French and English, and devoted to an international, progressive point of view. In one of the last issues, *Dyn* celebrates the liberation of Paris, hopefully declaring that it was "the end of a great mental eclipse, all becomes possible again!" But in the same issue, young Robert Motherwell wrote of the artist's possible relation to society in a decidedly pessimistic vein. Reflecting the painter's preoccupation with political idealism of the prewar period, he analyzes society with the disciplined approach of a Marxist. He relates modern art to the problem of the modern individual's freedom, and he doesn't think there is much chance of protecting individual freedom. He tries to make himself believe that "the modern artist tends to become the last active spiritual being in the great world" but he allows an ironic undertone to belie his faith. He heralds his own and the other artists' departure from class-conscious thought by saying "the materialism of the middle class and the inertness of the working class leave the modern artist without any vital connection to society save that of the *opposition.*"

The artist's opposition was, nevertheless, one positive

way of linking him to society. Society has long been tutored in the scientific notion of progress. At the same time a tribal respect for the artist has survived. On the one hand, society has been taught that the artist is "ahead" of the rest of us and, therefore, he represents progress. Even his "opposition" is taken as a sign of his advancement. On the other hand, the artist is "ahead" of us and therefore represents prophecy — not scientific prophecy based on empirical observation, but magical prophecy. The multiplication of pseudomystic and miraculous aesthetic theories which the artist's opposition engendered is symptomatic of a great spiritual hunger. Motherwell was right to conceive the artist's role as that of active spirituality.

To this spiritually starved society the contemporary artist becomes a sort of priest or shaman. His repeated gesture becomes the equivalent of a crucifix sign or the evil-eye sign. In this ritualistic mode the repeated sign can be accepted each time anew. A curious faith has been posited in contemporary painting and through it the viewer can feel gratified by repetition just as the orthodox Catholic is gratified by the unchanging aspects of an icon.

The shaman in many societies is described as the man who "sees." He "sees" not only in the occult sense, but is reputed to see great distances physiologically. The idea of illumination hangs about the shaman. His vision is expected to be more profound, synoptic. Like the contemporary painter, he is expected to move beyond the frontiers of ordinary sensory experience in order to envision microcosmic and macrocosmic forms. He is the community's cosmogonist.[1]

He is also the guardian of memory. He is responsible for the transmission of oral literature — the literature about the origin of humanity. He is the poet (in one culture he is described as having a vocabulary of 12,000 words while the rest of the community knows only 4000), the musician, priest, doctor and wise man. Above all, he is professionally hysterical. That is, he must have the courage and obsessive will to mortify himself, either psychologically or with the aid of drugs, in order to face the Unknown. He undertakes his ecstatic experiences on behalf of the community.

Part of the shaman's task, according to Mircea Eliade, is to rid his body of flesh and blood in such a way that only the bones remain. In ridding himself of that which is ephemeral and perishable, he goes symbolically to the netherworld of death in order to be resurrected a new man. The bones are the part of his body "destined to resist the longest time the action of the sun, winds and time."

The painter in making his signs and gestures, or series of signs and gestures, is also removing himself from calendar time, and from the frightening events in time that threaten his vision of a meaningful, unified cosmos. He feels obliged to take risks and it is expected of him that he be a professional hysteric.

The range of examples in the arts is very wide. Among writers, for example, it embraces the beatnik drugged poets as well as a solemn explorer like Henri Michaux whose recorded experiences with mescaline read like sociologists' reports on shamanism. Michaux, in the orthodox romantic tradition, sets out to disorient his senses and expose his self to the dangers of annihilation. Hoping for revelation, he travels to anonymous spaces. He experiences great "vibration" and an intuition of the absolute that he calls *extrêmement*. He travels as far from his normal human axis as possible and waits for his vision to become real. But when he calls his book *Misérable Miracle* he says a great deal, for in the end, without the support of his senses which mescaline diminishes, his experience is repetitive, lusterless, ultimately unilluminating. The great light of the infinite, artistically speaking, fails.

With painters the light has often failed too. Among the thousands of workers in the infinite, very few have had the miraculous experience, the height of jubilation known to the few. Some painters, especially among the younger generations, automatically imitate the shamans and avoid the trap of history and events (they may no longer read newspapers or worry about lynchings in the South) but fall instead into another trap: the trap of ritual.

I am not suggesting that the experience of the great cosmic spaces is invalid. When Tobey, Wols or Pollock went back to fundamentals and suggested cosmological analogies, they offered genuine experiences of great value. I am not discussing here individual painters and their value, but rather, the role of art in a society that knows great fear.

Fear and revulsion have played large parts in the formation of the arts in our century. Reactions of disgust recur regularly. It is surely significant that one of the strongest impulses has been to describe the absurd. Dada, born in the First World War and still flourishing, seems to be one of the artists' symmetrical responses to intolerable history. Surely the 5000 works of Dubuffet are in themselves a significant phenomenon. Such a production can only be thought of as miraculously absurd. The same can be said for all the do-it-yourself constructors such as Tinguely, Rauschenberg and a host of others who claim to use the debris of the world to represent the world.

Accent on the absurd, the somber, the desperate occurs not only in the visual arts but in music and writing as well. Speaking of the new electronic music, Theodor Adorno wrote that its purpose is to illuminate the absurdity of the world.[2] The new music "sacrifices itself to incomprehensibility. It has taken on itself all the darkness and sin of the world." In a singularly romantic passage, full of abstractions, Adorno says that the new music "finds its happiness in pointing to unhappiness; acquires all its beauty in denying the beautiful . . . sounds without being heard, without echo . . . is the experience of total isolation in forgetfulness . . . is a virtual bottle flung into the sea." The short-circuiting of communication is the major theme of those who have fled to the absurd, and we must take their flight as a serious commentary on the world.

In his fearful condition, the artist experiences a genuine thirst for myth. He knows that the record of passing events, the accumulation of observed facts in clock time, ultimately does not satisfy the human psyche. Human beings need to feel a freedom from history — their own and their collective history. The artist supplies that freedom by resurrecting myths which are the only human creations that escape the mortal strokes of Time. The recognition of the absurd serves an important function. Kunitz has said that art does not attack its age with its opposite, but applies homeopathic doses of what the age seems to be demanding until in the end the age dies of nausea.

The visual artist in recent years has not spoken of specific myths but has returned to grand cosmogonic themes that myths encompass: the primordial wildernesses, astral spaces, cavernous places where life was legendarily spawned, aqueous and subterranean depths that give birth to myths, the symbolic Center, the shelter ritually conse-crated. The contemporary painter — even he who is react-ing to informalism and tries to impose order of a rigorous kind in his work — is involved with mythmaking.

The danger to him is that of moving too far away from his own center. At first he is faithful to his experience, to the moment of illumination. But, after some time, he often begins to regard his image-making as a rite. He abandons the original cue and specific detail in his myth. Making a sign becomes the efficacious gesture and the form of the sign becomes secondary. Instinctively he seeks archetypes — the forms that symbolize experiences that are the same each time. Here he passes beyond myth and into the great swamp of abstraction.

Myths, after all, are always a mixture of the human and the superhuman. No miracle can occur without human error which produces the need for miracle. Birth, death, adultery, incest — the presence of these finite affairs en-ables the mythmaker to express their opposite. The stuff of myths is finite: a husband is unfaithful to his wife. The wife complains to her father. He, in a moment of divine rage, eclipses the husband in darkness. From this homely little tale of human error and weakness, the mythmaker is able to construe an expression of Infinite Darkness. But only dialectically, through flesh-and-blood example. No miracles can occur without the existence of the commonplace.

The artist often knows how to bring us to the brink of chaos, and how, at the critical moment, to express its opposite: form. It is a delicate matter of degree and scale and it is not always easy to determine who has been successful in wresting form from chaos. For instance, after Rothko's example, many younger artists adopted thin, filmy techniques, covering entire canvases with floats of color. Sometimes they have reduced their means to the mere covering of a canvas with a single color. They have thought they were expressing the infinite. Yet, how much more stirring is Miró's evocation of the infinite, with its singing blue sky traversed by a springy line and punctuated with two carefully placed spheres. Miró's dominant blue is infinite, but the line represents his hand tracing man's presence. It is the intimate detail, the reminder of a man's experiencing the infinite that tells of infinity. In short, Miró restores a dialectic, a certain visual logic to the unknown. He makes an image of chaos.

In primitive societies, myths are commemorated with the worship of matter itself. The most primitive African fetishes are made with crusts of dried blood, millet and mud. No one could claim for them more than their incantatory power of suggestion. They do not bear long contemplation and they do not open out complex possibilities.

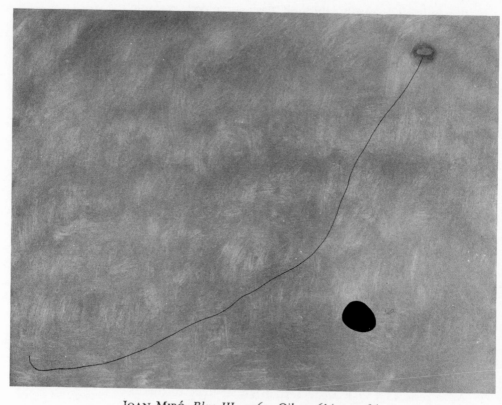

JOAN MIRÓ, *Blue III*, 1961. Oil, 106¼ x 139¾.

(Pierre Matisse Gallery, New York)

They tell of one side, one fearful side of man's psyche.
Perhaps this can be said of many contemporary paintings in which materials themselves are the subject.

In their way the African fetishes recall the chaos from which the world was formed. But everything in human spiritual life works toward a denial of chaos, even at its primitive level. To produce a form or an image is to fix Time. The painter who expresses infinity finally is the one who can express its opposite; who can, on the same canvas, give the finite measure of human experience and an intimation of its infinite measure.

The painter suffers the riddles of the cosmos intensely. He tries in his medium to lessen their chaotic pressure. To-day's painters question the universe with as much sober passion, as much desire to "see" ideal unity, as any artists in the past.

The contemporary artist sees himself in a tragic situation, a troubled man in a world whose mystery he can never satisfactorily penetrate. But he is not alone in history. Even so solid a figure as Goethe knew what it meant to follow a destiny in which the unforeseen lured him onward:

"One wonders how a man can bear to live another forty years in a world that even when he was young seemed to him void of meaning.

"The answer to part of the riddle is: because we each have something peculiarly our own that we mean to develop by letting it take its course. This strange thing cheats us from day to day, and so we grow old without knowing how or why. . . ."

Notes

AUTHOR'S NOTE: Where sources are thoroughly familiar or easily traced, I have omitted footnotes.

CHAPTER 1
1. Pierre Charles Baudelaire, review of 1859 Salon.
2. Gustave Flaubert, *Correspondance* (Paris, 1893, 4 vol.), Vol. III, p. 158.
3. Pierre Charles Baudelaire, *Edgar Poe, sa vie et ses oeuvres* (Paris: Lévy Frères, 1856).

CHAPTER 2
1. *The New American Painting,* Introduction by Alfred H. Barr, Jr., Mar. 1958. Catalogue published by the Museum of Modern Art for an exhibition of the work of seventeen American painters which traveled to eight European countries in 1958-1959.
2. Armory Show: New York, Feb. 1913. Arthur B. Davies and Walt Kuhn led a group of twenty-five artists to organize this exhibition of some 1600 works by more than 300 artists. Among Europeans represented for the first time with several works were Cézanne, Van Gogh, Gauguin, Redon and Matisse. Many American painters participated. The show remained open for an entire month and drew 100,000 people. Marcel Du-

champ's "Nude Descending a Staircase" was just one of the many items causing scandal and outrage.

3. Royal Cortissoz, *American Artists* (New York: Scribner's, 1923).

CHAPTER 3

1. William Carlos Williams, *In the American Grain* (New York: New Directions Paperback, 1956), p. 216.

2. Harold Rosenberg, *The Tradition of the New* (New York: Horizon Press, 1959), Chap. I, pp. 13-22.

CHAPTER 4

1. In 1936 a large group of artists banded together to form the American Abstract Artists' group. They have continued to exhibit together ever since.

2. John Cotton Dana, *American Art, How It Can Be Made to Flourish* (Woodstock, Vt.: Elmtree Press, 1914).

3. The full program of the Federal Arts Project under the WPA got under way in 1935 and died away in 1941.

4. Robert Motherwell, in report of the symposium "What Abstract Art Means to Me," published in Museum of Modern Art Bulletin, Vol. 15, No. 3, Spring, 1951.

5. Mark Rothko, statement in *The Tiger's Eye*, No. 9, Oct. 1949, p. 114.

6. Clyfford Still, from a 1952 letter quoted in *Fifteen Americans*, Museum of Modern Art catalogue, 1952, p. 22.

7. Summarized in *Modern Artists in America* (New York: Wittenborn, Schultz, 1951).

CHAPTER 5

1. *The New American Painting,* catalogue published by the Museum of Modern Art, Mar. 1958.

2. *Modern Artists in America,* p. 16.

3. Harold Rosenberg, "The American Action Painters," *Art News,* Dec. 1952.

4. Sören Kierkegaard, "That Individual," cited by Walter Kaufmann in *Existentialism from Dostoevsky to Sartre* (New York: Meridian, 1956), p. 97.

5. *Possibilities,* I, ed. by Robert Motherwell, John Cage, Harold Rosenberg, Pierre Chareau (New York: Wittenborn, Schultz, 1947-48).

6. Kaufmann, *Existentialism from Dostoevsky to Sartre.*

CHAPTER 6

1. Paul Klee, *Creative Credo* (Berlin, 1920).

2. Ernst Cassirer, *An Essay on Man* (Doubleday, 1953).

3. For biographical and other data on Gorky I am indebted to Ethel Schwabacher, who wrote the first book-length study, *Arshile Gorky* (New York, Macmillan, 1957).

4. Arshile Gorky, "Stuart Davis," *Creative Art,* Sept. 1931.

CHAPTER 7

1. Henri Focillon, *Maîtres de l'Estampe* (Paris: Laurens, 1930), in chapter entitled "Nouveau Monde," p. 159.

2. Mark Rothko, lecture at Pratt Institute, Oct. 1958, reported by me in the *New York Times,* Oct. 21, 1958.

3. Robert Motherwell, "The Creative Artist and His Audience," *Perspectives U.S.A.,* No. 9, Autumn, 1954.

4. Jack Tworkov, statement in *It Is,* Autumn, 1958, p. 15.

CHAPTER 8

1. Willem de Kooning, "The Renaissance and Order," *trans/formation,* Vol. I, No. 2, 1951, p. 86.

2. Alberto Giacometti, "Mai, 1920," *Moods and Movements in Art* (New York: Reynal, 1959), p. 33. First published in *Verve.*

CHAPTER 9

1. Louis Pauwels and Jacques Bergier, *Le Matin des Magiciens* (Paris: Gallimard, 1960), p. 12.

2. Arthur Waley, *Three Ways of Thought in Ancient China* (Garden City: Doubleday Anchor, 1956).

3. Jackson Pollock, in *Possibilities, I,* 1947-48.

4. Henry P. Bowie, *On the Laws of Japanese Painting* (New York: Dover), p. 48.

CHAPTER 10

1. Mark Tobey, excerpts from a letter dated Oct. 28, 1954, published in *The Art Institute of Chicago Quarterly,* Feb. 1, 1955, Vol. XLIX, No. 1, p. 9.

CHAPTER 11

1. Paul Klee, *Über die moderne Kunst* (Berne: Benteli, 1945).

2. For typical Tapié diction, and other items of interest, see *Phases,* No. 1, Editions Facchetti, 1954; *Phases,* No. 2, Editions Falaize, 1955.

3. André Breton, introduction to catalogue for Degottex, Galerie Kléber, Paris, 1955.

4. Piero Dorazio, *La Fantasia dell'Arte Nella Vita Moderna* (Rome: Polverone e Quinti, 1955), p. 143.

5. Among founding members of the Cobra group were Asger Jorn

of Denmark, Karel Appel and Corneille of Holland, and Pierre
Alechinsky of Belgium.

CHAPTER 12

1. Most of the quotations cited here are from *Prospectus aux Ama-
teurs de Tout Genre,* Dubuffet's book published by Gallimard
in 1946. Other statements may be found in the Dubuffet catalogue by Peter Selz published in the spring of 1962 by the
Museum of Modern Art.

2. André Pieyre de Mandiargues, *Jean Dubuffet: Le Point Extrême,*
Cahiers Musée de Poche, No. 2, June 1959, p. 52.

3. Marcel Raymond, *From Baudelaire to Surrealism* (New York:
Wittenborn, Schultz, 1950), p. 256.

4. Michel Ragon, *L'Aventure de l'Art Abstrait* (Paris: Laffont,
1956).

CHAPTER 13

1. Wols, quoted in catalogue for Dubuffet-Wols-Michaux exhibition, Studio Paul Facchetti, May 1957, in Paris.

CHAPTER 14

1. Northrup Frye, *Anatomy of Criticism* (Princeton: Princeton
University Press, 1957), p. 40.

CHAPTER 15

1. Quotes drawn from *Concerning the Spiritual in Art,* a translation of Kandinsky's *Über das Geistige in der Kunst* (1912),
published in New York by Wittenborn, Schultz, 1947.

2. Clement Greenberg, introduction to Hofmann catalogue for exhibition at Kootz Gallery, Jan. 1959.

3. Stanley William Hayter, "The Language of Kandinsky" in *Concerning the Spiritual in Art.*

CHAPTER 16

1. *Mallarmé: Selected Prose Poems, Essays and Letters,* translated
with an introduction by Bradford Cook (Baltimore: Johns Hop-
kins, 1956), p. 34.

2. Kandinsky, *Über das Geistige in der Kunst.*

3. John Cage, *Silence* (Wesleyan University Press, 1961).

4. Alfred H. Barr, Jr., *Picasso, Fifty Years of His Art* (New York:
Museum of Modern Art, 1946), p. 98.

5. Paul Rosenfeld, *An Hour with American Music* (Philadelphia:
Lippincott, 1929). Rosenfeld repeated his observations with
slight changes in several periodical articles.

6. Edgard Varèse, in catalogue for Michel Cadoret exhibition, New
York, Galerie Norval, Nov. 1960.

7. Frank O'Hara, jacket essay for *New Directions in Music/Morton Feldman,* Columbia Masterworks MS 6090. Significantly, O'Hara is better known as a poet and art critic than as a music commentator.

8. Henry Cowell, "Current Chronicle," *The Musical Quarterly,* Vol. XXXVIII, No. 1, Jan. 1952, pp. 123-136.

9. André Boucourechliev, "Qu'est-ce que la musique sérielle?" *France Observateur,* Aug. 31, 1961, p. 17.

CHAPTER 17

1. A. D'Abro, *The Evolution of Scientific Thought from Newton to Einstein* (New York: Dover, 1950).

2. Maurice Blanchot, *Le Livre à Venir* (Paris: Gallimard, 1959).

3. Gaston Bachelard, *La Poétique de l'Espace* (Paris: Presses Universitaires de France, 1957).

CHAPTER 18

1. Lancelot Law Whyte, "Some Thoughts on the Design of Nature and Their Implication for Education," address delivered at the International Design Conference, Aspen, Colorado, 1955, reprinted in *Arts & Architecture,* Vol. 73, No. 1, Jan. 1956.

2. D'Abro, *The Evolution of Scientific Thought from Newton to Einstein.*

3. Pauwels and Bergier, *Le Matin des Magiciens.*

4. Julien Alvard, "Antagonismes," catalogue essay published by the Musée des Arts Decoratifs, Feb. 1960.

5. Stéphane Lupasco, *Les Trois Matières* (Paris: Julliard, 1960).

6. Paul Valéry, *L'Idée Fixe* (Paris: Les Laboratoires Martinet, 1932).

CHAPTER 19

1. For a brilliant discussion of shamanism, see Mircea Eliade, *Mythes, Rêves et Mystères* (Paris: Gallimard, 1957), pp. 100-132.

2. Theodor Adorno, in *Philosophy of the New Music,* 1949, cited by Heinz-Klaus Metzger in "Hommage à Edgard Varèse," *Lettre Ouverte,* No. 3, Oct. 1961.

Index

Index